Seven Blessing Blockers

Evelyn Johnson-Taylor

Seven Blessing Blockers by Evelyn Johnson-Taylor
Copyright © 2008 Evelyn Johnson-Taylor

All rights reserved. No part of this publication may be reproduced, stored in a retrieval system, or transmitted in any form or by any means, electronic, mechanical, digital, photocopy, recording, or any other except for brief quotations in printed reviews, without the prior permission of the publisher.

Unless otherwise indicated, all Scripture quotations are taken from the HOLY BIBLE, NEW INTERNATIONAL VERSION ®. Copyright © 1973, 1978, 1984 by International Bible Society. Used by permission of Zondervan Publishing House. All rights reserved. Scriptures marked KJV are taken from the King James Version of the Bible. Scriptures marked ASV are taken from the American Standard Version of the Bible. Scriptures marked NLT are taken from the Holy Bible, New Living Translation, copyright © 2006. Used by permission of Tyndale House Publishers, Inc., Wheaton, Illinois 60189. All rights reserved. Scriptures marked NASB are taken from the New American Standard Bible®, Copyright © 1960,1962,1963,1968,1971,1972,1973,1975,1977,1995 by The Lockman Foundation. Used by permission. Scriptures marked NKJV are taken from the New King James Version. Copyright © 1982 by Thomas Nelson, Inc. Used by permission. All rights reserved.

ISBN 978-0-9908338-0-2
For Worldwide Distribution
Printed in the U.S.A.

Note: This is an updated and expanded version of Evelyn Johnson-Taylor's book entitled, Women of Promise.

Promise Publishing House
PO Box 46753, Tampa, FL 33646
info@promisepublishinghouse.com

Dedication

This book is dedicated
to my husband Scott,
my daughters Jade and Ebony,
and to my mother Annie Johnson.
I also would like to dedicate
this book in memory
of my father,
the late Bishop Martin
Luther Johnson Sr.
(1910-1990).

Table of Contents

Introduction   vii

Chapter 1. Become a Woman of Promise   1

Chapter 2. The Promises of God   10

Chapter 3. Unforgiveness   23

Chapter 4. Attitude   37

Chapter 5. Pride   47

Chapter 6. Fear   58

Chapter 7. Jealousy   73

Chapter 8. Self-Image   82

Chapter 9. Holding Onto the Past   97

Chapter 10. Test of Obedience   108

Study Guide Questions   120

Daily Devotional Readings   141

Introduction

Living a life of obedience can open the door to God's many blessing in your life. It is our heavenly Father's desire to shower His blessings upon us. Many times we allow things and issues to hold us back from where God wants to take us.

I will share with you my journey to obedience. It has not always been easy to obey, nor have I always obeyed. It is easy to think we know what is best and that we know more. I assure you I have had those thoughts at one time or another.

I have found in my own life that when I walk in obedience to God's Word, the promises of God flow freely into my life. It becomes a bit more challenging when I try to do things my own way. In fact, the more I try within my own strength, the more difficult it is to navigate the maze of life.

Our failure to obey the Word of God is the biggest obstacle that stands between us and our ability to reap the promises of God. It is our obedience that releases the promises of God into our lives.

My prayer for you is that you will be encouraged to turn your heart to obey God in every way and reap the promises of His Word. The Scripture teaches that if we are willing and obedient, we will eat the good of the land. Obedience has its rewards.

If the promises of God are to be evident in our lives, you must walk in total obedience. It is not enough for me to tell others what God has said, but each of us must apply the Word of God to our own lives first. When we walk according to the plan and purpose of God for our lives, other will see the fruit we produce.

During our lives, we often wonder if what we are doing is purposeful, and we want affirmation. I remember when I first knew I was fulfilling God's plan for my life. In the early days of my ministry, I led a women's Bible study group in our living room upstairs while my husband watched our daughters downstairs. (We had a big play area for our girls on the lower level of our home.)

My husband would also provide childcare for any woman who wanted to attend the women's Bible study. He would read the children a Bible story while I taught the women's Bible study class. It was there in my living room that my calling was affirmed when I saw each of these precious women move from a place of mediocrity to become a Woman of Promise.

It was through the teaching of God's Word that they were empowered to position themselves for blessings. Many years later, some of them are now in ministry leadership positions themselves and continue to inspire and challenge me to fulfill my destiny. I stand in awe of God's greatness when I see the impact these women have had on the lives of others.

It is imperative that each of us seek God's purpose for our lives. I am convinced that we will never know true joy until we begin to walk in purpose. Discovering our purpose requires that we spend time with God.

As we spend time in the Word of God, we will learn what God desires from us. The Scripture records in Micah 6:8, *"He has showed you, O man, what is good. And what does the Lord require of you? To act justly and to love mercy and to walk humbly with your God."* This verse speaks of the attitude that God requires when we come before Him to worship. The majority of the people of Israel had violated these standards.

Even today, God's desire is that we walk uprightly before

Him. When we walk uprightly, we are positioning ourselves for God's blessing. Do not let anything stand between you and what God has for you.

Perhaps, like the people of Israel, you have violated God's standards repeatedly. The Scripture tells us that we all have sinned and come short of God's glory (Romans 3:23). There is room for improvement in our lives. There are higher heights and deeper depths for us to obtain.

God's forgiveness is readily available to all who confess and believe. The abundant life that we read about in Scripture is available to anyone who will trust God. My challenge to you is to accept God's blessing for your life. I want to give you the keys to unlock the door to your blessings.

The *Seven Blessing Blockers* discussed in this book will set the groundwork for overcoming whatever hinders your blessing. Anything that blocks your blessing is considered a blessing blocker. The names may be different for many of us, but the results are the same.

If we want to receive God's promises, it is required that we live a life of commitment to God. If we want to move from a place of bondage to a place of freedom, obedience is necessary. Many times we remain in our wilderness because of our murmuring and complaining.

Let me teach you through the Word of God how to have the promises of God unleashed in your life. God's Word will show you how to walk into everything God has promised you, for each of us has been called by God to fulfill our purpose. In order to fulfill your purpose, you must strive to be obedient to the Word of God.

Chapter 1

Become a Woman of Promise

God's Word is filled with many great promises for our lives. The challenge for us is to have the promises manifested in our lives. The principles I will teach you in this book have set me free. I no longer live a life of fear, anxiety, and wondering if I am living God's plan.

I spent many years going through life hoping and wishing. Many times I wondered, *Am I doing what God wants me to do? Am I where God wants me to be?* I did not really know and felt as if I were guessing my way through life.

It has been a journey for me, but my lessons were well learned. Some were harder than others, and some took longer than others. God was waiting on me. Remember, the children of Israel's wilderness experience could have been much shorter; it was their disobedience, their murmuring, and their complaining that kept them wandering in the wilderness all those years.

Many times we live a life of disobedience, and we wonder why our plans are not working out for us. Instead of seeking to be obedient, we begin to complain about our situations. As we complain, circumstances grow worse, not better.

A life of obedience will be the turning point. Complaining will not change your situation. Its only reward is to make us feel worse about the situation in which we find ourselves. If our situations are to change, we must take a different approach. We cannot keep doing the same thing in our lives and expect a different result.

I am confident that my journey will help other women. I have always believed that everything God allows us to go through in our lives is for the purpose of helping others. I have walked through certain things that I had no idea I would have to deal with in my life. If people had told me thirty years ago about these experiences, I would not have believed them. There is a good reason we do not know our futures.

God reveals His plan for us step by step; if He showed us the entire plan all at once, we would not be able to handle it. If we could see what was around the corner, many of us (if not all) would turn back. What is behind us is maybe painful, but nevertheless, it is familiar.

What is in front may be better than what is behind, but we crave familiarity. Knowing what is going to happen is comforting. We are blessed to live in a time when we have the awesome advantage of seeing the results of what it means to obey God's Word. We read about many great men and women of the Bible who walked in obedience. We also have examples of those who disobeyed the Word of God.

In the midst of my life's challenges, one thing that has ringed constant for me is the purpose and plan of God for my life. As we walk through these seven blessing blockers, I want you to experience release and overflow in every area of your life. God has not forgotten you. You can trust a loving and all-knowing God with your life.

Become a Woman of Promise

As Christians, too often we live unfulfilled, unfocused, and nonpurposeful lives. We live in a world that sometimes seems void of hope. We experience wars, scarcity, and other forms of toxicity. Sometimes we get discouraged when we look at the prospects for our future.

While the economy may be saying one thing to us, God is saying another. While your circumstances may cry out hopelessness, God is saying that He has a plan to prosper and not harm you.

We were not meant merely to exist but to thrive. There is so much more for us to tap into so we can begin to reap the harvest. I challenge you to explore with me and gain an understanding of your purpose. God does have a plan for your life (He really does); and if you are like me, you want to know what it is.

Understanding God's plan and purpose for your life is really not that difficult. Your understanding of God's purpose is entangled with your relationship with Him. If you do not have a relationship with your heavenly Father, how can He communicate to you His plan for your life?

I believe that as you read this book, you will be released from everything that holds you captive. I want you to walk in the fullness of everything God has promised you. You do not have to settle for less than God's best. He wants to pour out so many blessings that you will not have enough room to receive them.

Begin to speak overflow in every area of your life and watch God perform at a level that may seem miraculous to you, but to God it is ordinary. The main way we can speak overflow in our lives is by our obedience to God. My former pastor used to say, "Talk is cheap." We cannot just claim the promises with our mouths and not walk in obedience.

You can live the abundant life and be fruitful. *"I have come that they may have life, and have it to the full"* (John 10:10). God wants you to enjoy your life and to walk in every promise He has given you in His Word. God does care; He is concerned about every little thing that concerns you. God is into details.

God loves us with an indescribable love. I thank God for loving me when I am viewed as unlovable by others. He loved me when I did not love myself. That is the awesomeness of God. How can anyone understand the love of an almighty God?

As you begin to seek Him for direction, know that we have His Word on it that He will show up to fulfill every promise in His Word. God is waiting for you to say, "Here I am, Lord, I am yours." I am convinced that God wants to pour out His blessings on His children. We must be in the right position to inherit the overflow.

God spoke to me concerning this at the beginning of the year 2005. He said, "Take the limits off of Me." God desires to show us more of His character and have His characteristics show up in us. We have put God in a box and limited Him in our lives. Do not limit God; ask large and watch Him answer your request.

God is big and He desires to do big things in our lives. *"Can you fathom the mysteries of God? Can you probe the limits of the Almighty?"* (Job 11:7). We must not limit the power and blessing of almighty God. Friends, He is a God of more: more joy, more favor, more blessings, more love, and more grace.

I have walked with God for nearly thirty-five years now, and each day I am more amazed by Him. He loves you and He loves me so very, very much. *"But God demonstrates his own love for us in this: While we were still sinners, Christ died for us"* (Romans 5:8). *"Give thanks to the God of gods. His love endures forever"* (Psalm 136:2).

As we walk in obedience to what God has asked us to do, we grow closer to Him. *"But if anyone obeys his Word, God's love is truly made complete in him. This is how we know we are in him"* (1 John 2:5). God desires to be intimate with His children. He wants to do for us what no other power can do.

There is absolutely nothing too hard for God. *"Is anything too hard for the Lord?"* (Genesis 18:14). God desires to do in our lives what may appear to be impossible to us. Jesus looked at them and said, *"With man this is impossible, but with God all things are possible"* (Matthew 19:26). *"For nothing is impossible with God"* (Luke 1:37). *"Jesus replied, What is impossible with men is possible with God"* (Luke 18:27).

I love being connected to a God who never fails. Man will let you down over and over again. God never fails; He will never let you down. He is faithful to fulfill His Word always. I marvel at the handiwork of His hands. Just when I think, "God you are awesome," He shows Himself even more faithful.

Friends, in my own life I have seen God work supernaturally doing what seemed impossible to me. He has proven Himself to be God all by Himself. God is ready to show Himself faithful to you and anyone who trusts in Him.

In Scripture God offers us a foolproof way of proving Him, *"Bring the whole tithe into the storehouse, that there may be food in my house. Test me in this, says the Lord Almighty, and see if I will not throw open the floodgates of heaven and pour out so much blessing that you will not have room enough* for it" (Malachi 3:10). I love this translation (NIV) of this Scripture. When I think of "throw open," I think of a door that cannot be easily closed. Sometimes when you throw open a door, the hinges are damaged in the process, and the door never closes tightly again. Praise God for the open door that will remain open as long as we continue to obey.

He gives us a condition and, as long as we meet the condition, we have His Word on it. This Scripture speaks of tithes and offerings, but I also believe it speaks to the relationship God desires to have with us. He wants us to know we can trust Him; when God's Word makes a statement, you can rely on the validity of that Word.

Moses could not enter the Promised Land because of disobedience and a lack of trust. *"But the Lord said to Moses and Aaron, Because you did not trust in me enough to honor me as holy in the sight of the Israelites, you will not bring this community into the land I give them"* (Numbers 20:12).

We must be willing and obedient to do whatever God has said. We do not want to miss out on the promises of God for our lives. Our ability to reap the promises depends on our willingness to obey the principles.

God will be to you what you allow Him to be. Do you want Him to be the God of just enough or the God of more than enough? He can just meet your needs or He can do exceeding abundantly above your needs. (Read Ephesians 3:20.) You can rejoice because you know that neither God's power nor His love is limited.

God wants to bless us beyond measure, but we must walk in obedience. The question is, how much do we want to be blessed? It is our choice; what are we waiting for? We have to take the limits off God. We do this by obeying Him. When we are obedient, we release God to perform every promise of His Word.

Some would accuse me of being too strict in my teaching, but I am convinced that our lifestyles must conform to God's

Word if we want to walk in the perfect will of God for our lives. Once we accept Jesus Christ as our personal Savior, things will change. Our desire will be to please Him in all that we do. Walking in obedience to God is a lifelong process.

Spiritual growth is indeed a progression; for some it is longer than for others. Some have rapid growth, and some have slow growth; nevertheless, growth must take place. If we are to follow the will of God for our lives, we must be constantly growing. *"But grow in the grace and knowledge of our Lord and Savior Jesus Christ. To him is glory both now and forever! Amen"* (2 Peter 3:18).

Over the years, the *method* for teaching Scripture has changed, and it must change. As a Bible teacher for a numbers of years, I am well aware of the many different women with whom I come in contact. The *message*, however, remains the same. If we want to walk in the fullness of our blessing, we must obey the Word of God.

We have to be committed to obedience in every area of our lives. Sometimes we will miss the mark, but we must keep trying; we cannot give up. Our God is gracious and merciful. He is patient with us, because He wants us to receive His blessings.

We can stand on the truth of His Word. *"So is my Word that goes out from my mouth: It will not return to me empty, but will accomplish what I desire and achieve the purpose for which I sent it"* (Isaiah 55:11). If God said it, then it is settled, whether we believe it or not. When we start to doubt the promises of His Word, it is His Word that encourages us.

We have to stand on what God has said. When we agree with God and believe and trust in His Word, nothing can stop us. Search the Scriptures, see and agree with what God has said, and then act on it.

Do not look at your circumstance or the situation; keep your eye on the promises of His Word. You cannot look at your problems with your natural eyes. It may look impossible, but with God, nothing is impossible.

Trust God. Do not place your trust in your own abilities, for you will be disappointed every time. *"Trust in the Lord with all your heart and lean not on your own understanding; in all your ways acknowledge him, and he will make your paths straight"* (Proverbs 3:5-6).

My walk with God has not always been easy; there have been some disappointments. Yes, there have been times I have felt like giving up (let's keep it real). But if you asked me what I know for sure, I know without a shadow of a doubt that God is faithful. You can depend on Him; if His Word said it, He will perform it.

God is usually not early, but He will show up on time. I would often hear my mother say, "He may not come when you want Him, but He is always on time." I really did not understand the full concept of that statement as a child. I now realize that when you have a need, anytime is a good time for the need to be met.

I challenge you to cry out to God and ask Him to draw you closer. As you are drawn closer, listen to His voice as He speaks to you. God desires a deeper, more personal relationship with you. My prayer is that you will be motivated to move into a place of obedience concerning God's will and purpose for your life.

Let's get ready to go to the next level in God. There is so much He wants to put within our grasp. When we open our heart to obedience, we open our hands to receive the blessing. God's love for us runs deep, and He wants to show us just how much He loves us.

I challenge you to be a student of the Word of God. God's Word is what changes the hearts and lives of people. Please pray as you read this book and allow God's Word to change your heart.

I can share my experiences and my faith with you, but ultimately it is the Word of God that moves you into position to be a receiver of the promises.

Chapter 2

The Promises of God

God's Word is filled with promises for those who walk in obedience. Too often we focus on the promises but overlook the principles He wants us to follow. We cannot violate the principles of God and expect to reap the promises from God. He is a God of order, and He cannot go against His Word. If we want to be blessed in our lives, we must follow God's order. *"But everything should be done in a fitting and orderly way"* (1 Corinthians 14:40).

If you want to reap a harvest, you must first put a seed in the ground. *"Remember this: Whoever sows sparingly will also reap sparingly and whoever sows generously will also reap generously"* (2 Corinthians 9:6). So I ask you, do you want some of the promises of God, or do you want everything God has promised you? I want it all; I want everything that is mine and more. God desires to bless us abundantly; He is the God of more than enough, the God of overflow.

When you go to God in prayer, you go believing for answers, right? You seek Him desiring a harvest. You want something in return for your prayer. Some of us desire spiritual blessings, and others desire natural ones.

The Promises of God

A question we need to ask ourselves when we go to God in prayer is, "What am I bringing to the Lord? Am I going to the Lord in obedience, knowing I have done what God has asked me to do? Or am I going expecting, when I am in violation of God's Word?" You cannot plead promises and violate principles; that will not work.

There are many who would have us believe that God is a Sugar Daddy or a Santa. Well, even Santa Claus wants to know if we have been naughty or nice before he leaves gifts under the tree. You have to leave a tooth under your pillow, or the tooth fairy will not leave you anything. I am not suggesting that God is a fairy godmother, but what I want you to understand is that there are conditions for receiving—yes, even from God.

He is a merciful God, and we should thank God for His love and mercy. Without the mercies of our heavenly Father, we would all perish. It is because of His great love for us that He gave His son Jesus to die for our sins. *"For I will forgive their wickedness and will remember their sins no more"* (Hebrews 8:12). But while He is merciful, He is also a just God. *"And sang the song of Moses the servant of God and the song of the Lamb: Great and marvelous are your deeds, Lord God Almighty. Just and true are your ways, King of the ages"* (Revelation 15:3).

When we come to God, we must ask for forgiveness. *"If I had cherished sin in my heart, the Lord would not have listened; but God has surely listened and heard my voice in prayer"* (Psalm 66:18-19). Here we see a condition for God hearing our prayers. We must not hold sin in our hearts but be quick to forgive.

We must not allow any sin or any person to stand between us and God's promises for us. God wants to meet all of our needs and fill us with great joy, but we must do our part.

God has requirements that His people are expected to meet, for He has standards that we are expected to uphold. And while it is true we cannot do it on our own, our heavenly Father remains willing and ready to help us.

When God put us here on earth to learn our lessons and to grow up spiritually, He did not intend that we should take over the school and change the requirements to suit ourselves. Whether we understand them or not, we have conditions to meet. Sometimes we may not agree with the conditions, but we are still required to follow the plan.

When your conscience tells you to stop, do not rationalize your curiosity. If Eve had just followed God's instructions, the world would be a different place today. Always remember that God is for you and that He is on your side; He desires to help you discover and fulfill your destiny.

God would never give us an assignment and leave us to carry it out alone. He is always present to help us when we call Him. He has not designed us to fail but to prosper. This bears repeating—God is for us, and He is always cheering for us. He wants us to not only to finish, but also to win.

We have appetites over which we have to take control; we cannot indulge in every desire if we expect to reap the promises. Sometimes we want things we cannot have. As believers, we cannot say yes to every pleasure. God has called us and set us apart for His glory. *"Before I formed you in the womb I knew you, before you were born I set you apart; I appointed you as a prophet to the nations"* (Jeremiah 1:5). Just as God knew Jeremiah, He knows us and knew us before we were formed in our mother's womb. We have been chosen by God for a specific purpose; we are divinely designed.

The law put certain "do not's" and "thou shalt not's" in our lives. If you want to walk in the fullness of God, you need to follow the instructions of His Word. You cannot disregard what God has asked you to do and expect to be blessed.

God has carefully planned the events of your life to bring you to where He needs you to be. *"Then my enemies will turn back when I call for help. By this I will know that God is for me"* (Psalm 56:9). Just as God was present in David's time of need, He will be present for you. God does not change; He changes circumstances, but He remains the same.

When you feel like giving up, let me assure you that God is for you. He is not against you; He is on your side. When you are obedient to follow His Word, He will not turn His back on you. You can always depend on God even when others let you down.

In my life there have been times when I thought others had me covered and had my back. Many of those times I found myself standing alone with no one on whom I could depend. It was at those times God would gently whisper to me, "I will cover you." Thank God for His covering over us.

> *If the Lord had not been on our side let Israel say; if the Lord had not been on our side when men attacked us, when their anger flared against us, they would have swallowed us alive; the flood would have engulfed us, the torrent would have swept over us, the raging waters would have swept us away* (Psalm 124:1-5).

No matter what obstacle you may be facing today, God is a very present help in the time of trouble. It is so good to know that God is on your side. In the darkest of night, God is right there; He will never leave you. He promised in His Word that He would never leave you nor forsake you (Hebrews 13:5). He is a God who keeps His Word.

Our society has become so accepting of everything. No

one wants to follow the rules anymore. We are raising a generation of young people who think anything goes. Parents, let me caution you: our children crave structure in their lives. They want someone to set limits for them; they want a parent, not another friend. Children do not have the ability to set limits for themselves. Parents, our children have enough friends. What they need are role models.

We live in a day where no one wants to be known as the strict parent. Neither Mom nor Dad wants to be the bad guy. Everyone wants to know, "Why can't we just be friends?" When our children grow up and have no respect for rules, then we want to scream and shout at them. We must remember that when we fail to deposit into them what is necessary for them to thrive, the unacceptable behaviors that result are not their fault. Let me assure you, Mom and Dad, that when we have done our part, we can trust God to do His part.

My teenage daughter asked me one day, "Mom, don't you want us to be friends like some of my friends are with their parents?" My reply was "No, I am your mother first and foremost. God has entrusted you to me to train you." I was not and am not confused by my role as her mother. My responsibility is to set limits in her life and to see that she follows the rules.

Our children today have a need to understand everything. The most frequently used word in their vocabulary is "why." Whenever a parental decision is made, they want to know why. While I believe parents should try to give their children an explanation, I do not believe it is obligatory. God has given each parent the responsibility of training his or her children. The child's understanding is not a prerequisite, but the parental training is necessary if we are to be obedient to the Word of God.

Friends will not always hold us accountable; sometimes

they want to play along with us. Parents, we have to hold our children accountable and encourage them to do what is right. We have to stand in the gap for our children.

Our children are our greatest investment. If we invest little in our children, the returns will be small. If we invest much in our children, we can stand on God's promise.

"Train a child in the way he should go, and when he is old he will not turn from it" (Proverbs 22:6). There is a principle here that Solomon teaches us. This Scripture instructs us that if we teach our children, the education will last throughout their lives.

My brother, who is now a pastor, came to know Jesus some years after our father went home to be with the Lord. This promise was not fulfilled in our father's lifetime, but God's Word is true. My brother testifies that because he was trained in the way he should go, he could not turn away from what he was taught. Our parents, both ministers of the Gospel, obeyed Proverbs 22:6.

Parents, we have God's Word that if we are obedient to do what He has asked us to do in the rearing of our children, they will not depart from the teachings. Any decision to come to the Lord is a personal choice they will have to make.

If we want to be obedient to the Word of God, then we as parents must guide our children, discipline them, and encourage them to choose the right path. I remember many of the lessons my parents taught me in childhood, many of which I am sure have led me to make the choices I make even today as a middle-aged adult.

I thank God for godly parents who were willing to be the horrific parents my siblings and I thought they were at the time. They were parents who did not seek the popularity of their children but were committed to obeying God.

Seven Blessing Blockers

When we are in a covenant relationship with our heavenly Father, we can depend on His favor. God is sovereign, and He can do what He wants to when He wants to do it. He can pick and choose whom to bless and whom not to bless. But as believers, we have a right to certain privileges just because we have a covenant with the Father. Our covenant agreement affords us certain privileges.

When you get married to your mate, you have certain expectations. Just because you are married to your spouse, you have the right to expect certain things. You can expect that person to love and respect you. You can expect them to honor and cherish you. Even if your spouse fails to act in this manner, the expectation remains because of the covenant the two of you made.

When you stand before God and agree to love, honor, cherish, and respect each other, both parties are expected to fulfill their end of the agreement. I am aware that this is not always the result, but that does not mean it should not be an expectation. The point I am trying to make is that covenant agreements sometimes are broken.

With the rising divorce rates and the number of people who are in unhappy marriages, I know the promises we make to each other on our wedding day are not always kept. We have good intentions; no one stands on their wedding day planning to divorce. Circumstances happen beyond our control, situations we did not anticipate. Things happen for which we have no point of reference; often we feel there are no guidelines or rule books for reference. God is our strength when everyone else fails us; He will not fail.

The God we trust is still faithful even in our disappointments. He loves us and cares for us always. His love is never ending. In fact, *"For God so loved the world that he gave his one and only Son that whoever believes in him shall not perish but have eternal life"* (John 3:16). Even before we entered into a right relationship with Him, He loved us. His love is the one thing that is unconditional; we can always count on the love of God.

I remember standing with my knees shaking when the bishop asked me if I would love, respect, and honor my husband-to-be. He asked me if I could commit even in sickness and health. He went on to say, for richer or for poorer, until death do you part. The more he talked the more nervous I became. With every word from the pastor's mouth, I thought, *Can I do this?*

We are asked to make a lot of promises on that special day. I was holding my breath, knowing I was not only promising my husband-to-be, but I was promising God. Then I heard the bishop say my answer, "With the help of God I will," I was able to breathe again and proclaim boldly, "With the help of God I will." I understood, even on that day, that I needed God. On my own, I would fail; but with God's help, I could do all things through Christ who would give me the strength.

Seventeen years later, I can tell you there have been many times I have had to say, "God, I need your help." He has never let me down. He always shows up to fulfill His part of the agreement. When we refuse to abide by our covenant agreements that we make to each other, God is faithful to fulfill His covenant agreement He makes to each of us. He is always dependable; He never falls short of His promises.

God is not like man; He keeps His Word. *"Heaven and earth will pass away, but my words will never pass away"* (Matthew 24:35). God will fulfill His covenant agreement with us.

God is not a man, that he should lie, nor a son of man that he should change his mind. Does he speak and then not act? Does he promise and not fulfill? I have received a command to bless; he has blessed, and I cannot change it (Numbers 23:19-20).

In other words, God will not go back on His Word. Actually, He cannot go back on His Word because He does not lie. He will stand by His covenant agreement. Anything God has promised, rest assured, He will fulfill. There is nothing lacking in God; when we line up with His Word, we can have it all.

We read in Deuteronomy 28 about the blessings of obedience and the curses of disobedience. A covenant is an agreement or pledge sealed between two or more parties. Notice there are two sides involved in a covenant. When we ask Jesus Christ to forgive us of our sins, the relationship has been restored. Sin destroyed the relationship between God and His people. Jesus Christ came to die to bridge the gap and to restore what had been broken by sin. The restored relationship put us in a covenant agreement. Sure, we mess up and make mistakes, but thank God for His mercies. *"Because of the Lord's great love we are not consumed, for his compassions never fail. They are new every morning; great is your faithfulness"* (Lamentations 3:22-23).

In this book, I will share with you seven things I believe hinder the promises of God from flowing into our lives. I want to focus on these seven because I believe if we can master these, the others will not be a problem. The same principles and skills you use to conquer these seven can be applied to any challenging area in your life.

God has already given you authority over every obstacle that seeks to prevent you from fulfilling the call of God on your life. As you pray, ask God to show you the blockers to your blessings. I believe you can conquer every one of them with the help of our heavenly Father. Once the problem has been identified, God's Word provides the solution.

It is time for believers to break free and walk in liberty. God has given us the power to pull down every stronghold in our lives.

> *For though we live in the world, we do not wage war as the world does. The weapons we fight with are not the weapons of the world. On the contrary, they have divine power to demolish strongholds. We demolish arguments and every pretension that sets itself up against the knowledge of God, and we take captive every thought to make it obedient to Christ* (2 Corinthians 10:3-5).

God's desire is that we break free from whatever holds us captive. Friends, when we can truly trust God, it is indeed a freeing experience.

Many things in our lives can hinder us and slow down the flow of God's promises. Anything that stands in the way of our obedience to God is considered a hindrance and will make the promises difficult to obtain. The word *hinder* in Greek means, "to put up a stumbling block, to miss a set appointed time, or to move away from your destined state."

The seven blessing blockers can block or hold back the promises and move you away from your destined state. I do not want you to miss your moment, your appointed time. The promises can be delayed simply because you are not fulfilling our end of the covenant agreement. The devil cannot stop the plan of God, but he can hinder it. As you move toward your destiny, the enemy will send a season of struggle to take you off focus.

That season of struggle can be physical, emotional, or financial. These are just some of the ways I have seen the enemy operate in the lives of believers to cause them to lose sight on the major goal. Anytime satan can cause you to focus on something else more than you focus on God, he has accomplished his goal.

My prayer for you is that you will have a supernatural release in your life right now. I believe that you are being set free from every device the enemy has devised to hinder your progress. I declare to you this day, you will reap every promise of God's Word as you walk in obedience. *"O Lord, open my lips, and my mouth will declare your praise"* (Psalm 51:15). What are you declaring? Start declaring overflow in every area of your life. Start declaring what you want in your life, but more importantly, make sure your walk is one of obedience.

When we make a vow, we are required to keep it. A vow binds us to an act, service, or condition. We are held accountable for the vows we make. When we are not experiencing the promises, we need to ask ourselves, "Have I kept my vow?" The failure is not in God; the failure is in us. We have only ourselves to blame for the failures we experience. Our heavenly Father is always ready to meet our needs; His deepest desire is to bless us and to favor us. He is waiting for us to get into position so the blessings can flow.

If you truly desire to be in covenant with your heavenly Father, begin to do what you know is right. As you read the Word, ask God to show you what else you should be doing. If you have difficulty understanding the Word, pray and ask God for revelation. Ask a spiritual leader or a trusted friend who is a believer to help you understand God's Word. God has strategically placed people in each of our lives to help us grow in Him. When you listen to the spoken Word, ask God to give you an open heart to receive the Word.

You may not know everything, but do what you know is right to do. Spend time with God on a daily basis, praying and listening for His voice. He will reveal to you the right things to do. Be obedient as He reveals things to you, and ask Him to show you the things in your life that are contradictory to His Word. As He shows them to you, begin to correct those areas of your life. God will help you to do this; you cannot do it on your own. When you start to obey in one area, God will speak to you about other areas. If you are not obedient in the area He shows you, why would He show you other areas?

The process of obedience can be painful; the flesh wants to have its way. As you die to the things of the flesh, God will restore and rebuild your life in such a way that it will be whole. Nothing will be missing, and nothing will be broken. God's desire for us is to have nothing lacking.

He wants to full every empty place in our hearts. Every believer can experience the fullness of life from a loving God. Once we commit our lives to follow Christ and obey His Word, our lives can be full. I am not saying our lives will be perfect, but I am saying that God will never fail us. I speak from my own experiences as I walk out the plan of God for my life.

In Ephesians 1:9-11 the Apostle Paul gives us some encouraging news.

> *And he made known to us the mystery of his will according to his good pleasure, which he purposed in Christ, to be put into effect when the times will have reached their fulfillment to bring all things in heaven and on earth together under one head, even Christ. In him we were also chosen, having been predestined according to the plan of him who works out everything in conformity with the purpose of his will.*

God is ever conscious of His thoughts, His counsel, and His eternal plan with respect to you. His thoughts toward you are not simply written in a file and tucked away; they are ever on His mind. The verses above teach that God's will is no longer a mystery. The will of God is revealed to those who walk in obedience. God has arranged all of history to fulfill His plan in regards to you. God is thinking so much about you that He arranges all things around you and provides for all your needs.

Every believer is always before the mind of the eternal God. Never has anything happened to a child of God that has not passed through the hands of a loving and wise God. There is no debate or question in God; He knows the promises He has made. He does not forget us. He remembers His covenant. He knows and is concerned about those who are His.

Nothing can take God by surprise, as He knows all. His thoughts toward us are settled and binding. The word predestinate simply means that God has a plan for us. Even before we were born, God had a plan for our lives. He finished us before He started us. God is truly awesome.

Now let's look at some of the areas that can hold us back from walking out the plan God has for our lives. When we do not follow the plan of God for our lives, we hinder the blessings of God in our lives.

Chapter 3

Unforgiveness

The ability to forgive has been a constant struggle for me over the years. Just when I thought I had forgiven, the same issues would arise again. It was like a bad taste in my mouth that would not go away. You drink glass after glass of liquid, but you just cannot get rid of the sour taste in your mouth. The incident would be different, but the challenge would be the same. Let me tell you, until you forgive, your life will be miserable. Life will pass you by if you are holding onto old offenses.

I have tried within my own abilities to forgive people who have hurt me. In some cases, I thought I was successful, only to realize that forgiveness was not something I would be able to accomplish on my own.

It has required much prayer on my part to be able to practice forgiveness. I had to rely on God to help me. In some cases, even today, it remains a daily challenge for me to let something remain in the past and to focus on what is ahead.

Some people I have no problem forgiving, while others it becomes a little more difficult. One of my issues has been that if certain people wrong me, I would hold onto the anger for a long time. I knew God was not pleased, but I just could not forgive certain ones; I felt they should have known better.

Many times, we show more compassion for strangers then we do for those close to us. It seems at times that I can put up with a lot from people to whom I am not close. If my husband or someone else close to me committed the same act, it is often a different story.

God requires us to forgive each and every person who has offended us. We do not get to pick and choose whom we will forgive and whom we will not forgive. In most cases, it is easier said then done, but God will never ask us to do anything that we cannot achieve with His help.

I had to allow the Word of God to change my thought process. *"Do not conform any longer to the pattern of this world, but be transformed by the renewing of your mind. Then you will be able to test and approve what God's will is—his good, pleasing and perfect will"* (Romans 12:2). We will need to rely on the strength that comes from God in order to forgive. If we are honest, we have to admit there is no way we can master forgiveness on our own.

As much as we need the help of God to make it through the day, we need Him more to help us to let go of past offenses and forgive. The mere fact that God has asked us to forgive our offenders affirms to me that He will help me to achieve this difficult task.

Knowing that God's help was readily available allowed me to seek Him diligently. Many nights I would lie in my bed crying out to God to help me. I knew I needed to forgive, but I just could not seem to muster up the energy to do it. I would rationalize why I was right, and they were wrong. Friend, it is not about being right or wrong; it is about being obedient. There was a war going on inside of me between the flesh and spirit. The flesh was saying, "Hold onto the grudge, cut them out of your life." The spirit of God in me was saying, "Let it go." I could not release the anger without the help of an almighty, loving God. In the midst of my tears, God was saying, "Forgive, if you want to be blessed." *"Do not repay evil with evil or insult with insult, but with blessing, because to this you were called so that you may inherit a blessing"* (1 Peter 3:9).

The people, who had offended me, in my eyes, did not deserve my time or attention; I wanted nothing further to do with them. I had been wounded so badly by the hands of those who stood with me, or so I thought. Holding onto anger, as I soon discovered, was more detrimental to me than to the ones who had hurt me. I was holding up my blessings and not fulfilling the call of God on my life. I was living so far outside of God's will for my life that I did not understand God's purpose for it. The plan that God has for us is always bigger than what we plan for ourselves. *"Great are your purposes and mighty are your deeds. Your eyes are open to all the ways of men; you reward everyone according to his conduct and as his deeds deserve"* (Jeremiah 32:19). I knew I would not allow unforgiveness to cause me to abort my destiny. I had to be obedient to what God was asking me to do. It would not be easy, but I understood that it would be possible with the love and help of my heavenly Father.

It did not feel good to the flesh to let it go, but if I wanted to walk in the promises, I had no choice. My flesh wanted to hold onto the negative feeling and forever avoid the ones who had hurt me. I was not able to forgive my offenders immediately; it was a process.

This journey took days, weeks, and in some cases years. I pray that it will not take you as long as it took me, but I do want to encourage you. God is ready, willing, and able to free you from everything that holds you back from the promises of

His Word. Even when you feel like you cannot forgive, know that with God's help you can.

For years, I repeated the same conversation with God in my head. Often I was reminded of what the Word of God said, yet I lived in disobedience. When we live a life of disobedience, we are in direct violation of the Word of God. When we are in violation of the Word of God, we cannot expect to live the abundant life that Christ promised us. The fact that I have a good memory is no excuse. Christ has taught us in Scripture that we must forgive.

Many times we do not want to let the offenses go. We want to hold onto them as a defense against succumbing to the same transgression again. We often think that if we keep our guard up no one will hurt us again. The truth is, life is filled with heartache and disappointments. We must learn to release all of our cares to a loving Father.

If you hold onto hurt, you are only hurting yourself. Many times the offenders have no memory of the offense. They are going on with their lives, and you are stuck in the past.

I, like many of you, was not ignorant concerning God's Word. I knew if I was to be used by God to the fullest, I would need to forgive. I would have to realize that God sees all and regardless of the situation, He still said forgive.

There are so many ways God wants to use us for His glory. He wants to trust us with His anointing. We as believers have to seek God's will for our lives. We must be willing to lay aside anything that hinders us from walking in obedience.

I would tell myself, "I have forgiven them." Just when I would think I had made it, I would get knocked back down. God was teaching me that I could not do this on my own and that I needed His help. I had to learn to depend on Him for everything because trusting in my own abilities would be a disaster, as I would surely fail.

Unforgiveness

The struggle to forgive is one we face on a daily basis. It can be difficult to overcome resentment, anger, and bitterness toward those who have hurt you. I am by no means proud of the fact I lived in disobedience so long. I knew what the Word of God said, but I was not practicing it. In many cases, I was teaching forgiveness but not committed to making it a reality in my life.

There are many others like me who are well acquainted with God's Word but are not putting it into practice. I share this to help you understand that you are not alone in your struggle to obey God's Word.

When my husband would do or say things that would upset me, I would walk around frustrated for days. He would tell me I had a memory like an elephant, whatever that means. While my feelings in most cases were valid, I could not be the Holy Spirit in his life. God would have to deal with him just as He was dealing with me. I knew he would have to give an account to God just as I would for my actions. When I relieved myself of the need to be his conscience, I felt liberated.

When you marry the right person, I believe God has placed that person in your life to help bring your issues to the surface so the issues can be dealt with appropriately. God knew I had a problem forgiving, so He gave me a husband who would give me plenty of practice. The funny thing is that it was not always my husband's actions that caused me to be frustrated; it was my perception of his actions.

The fact that men and women do not think alike is no secret. Both parties can hear the same statement but interpret it differently. That is the beautiful way our God has made us. When we learn to appreciate each other's differences, life can be great. The plan of God for our lives encompasses our whole life, including our marriages and how we relate to each other.

My struggles and issues can only bring glory to God when I

use them to help others. I allowed the actions of others to keep me confined in my own prison of anger and resentment. I did not realize it at the time, but I was slowly dying both physically and spiritually. Only God would see my heart, and only He knew what I was really feeling.

I spent years feeling betrayed, and I was obsessed with a "why me?" attitude. When the action of others would hurt me, I would adopt the role of the victim instead of the role of the victor. I tried to live a good life and did not really bother others, so why were they bothering me? I kept circling the same mountain over and over. I would take two steps forward thinking, "I have the victory this time," only to find myself falling backward into the same old way of thinking.

Once I really got it and understood what I needed to learn, it all made sense. There was a lesson I had to learn, something God needed me to understand once and for all. God was saying to me, "You have to learn to forgive, really forgive." I then realized the reason God provided so many opportunities for me to forgive was because I had not learned to forgive. If you and I want to fulfill the call of God on our lives, we must learn to forgive.

I now know that my years in darkness were of my own choosing. I had a three strike rule: you hurt me one time, no problem; you hurt me the second time, we can get past it; but if you hurt me a third time, that was it. Yes, I kept a record of the number of times I felt misused. Thank God He does not have that same rule. I have messed up so many times, yet He continues to love me.

The issue you resist most is usually the issue God wants to perfect in you so you can help others. The reason it takes so long for God to bring about the change in us is because we give God the issue and then we take it back. We give it to Him again and then take it back again. It is ironic that we wonder

Unforgiveness

why we keep having the same issues over and over; it is because we have not learned the lesson.

Once we learn the lesson, then it is really over. I am grateful we serve such a loving and patient God. He does so much more than just work with us on our issues. He will use the same issue we dealt with and allow us to help somebody else who is struggling so that person can also overcome.

Your deliverance is not a testimony until you can tell somebody about it. So many times we fail to use our experiences to help others. The trials you go through are not just for you, but they are so you can help others to obtain the same victory you now enjoy.

We can hinder the flow of God's promises by harboring unforgiveness in our hearts. The Bible uses the word forgiveness many times. *"But if you do not forgive men their sins, your Father will not forgive your sins"* (Matthew 6:15). *"Bear with each other and forgive whatever grievances you may have against one another. Forgive as the Lord forgave you"* (Colossians 3:13).

Forgiveness is the key to breaking free from your past hurts and disappointments. To forgive is to absolve, pardon, or cease to feel resentment against an offender. When every fiber in your body wants to hold onto the feelings of hurt and pain, God is saying, "Forgive so I can fill that place of pain with joy." *"Be kind and compassionate to one another, forgiving each other, just as in Christ God forgave you"* (Ephesians 4:32).

God's Word is our book of instructions; we must be obedient to what we are asked to do. I understood how important forgiveness was by reading God's Word. *"And when you stand praying, if you hold anything against anyone, forgive him, so that your Father in heaven may forgive you your sins"* (Mark 11:25). Many times, we come before God with requests but neglect to ask God to help us to forgive those who have done us wrong.

There have been many instances in my life where I felt I was dealt a raw deal. It just did not seem to be fair that I had to be treated in such a rude way. I must forgive the ones who I feel have betrayed me, and not just once, for forgiveness is continuous.

When my flesh tells me I cannot forgive this time, I have to remind myself that I have hurt others and am in need of their forgiveness. More importantly, I need God's forgiveness. If I cannot forgive my offender, God will not forgive me.

Forgiveness is not a one-time act. Every time you remember the offense, you have to forgive again and again. God has truly helped me in such a way that when I am in the presence of a person who has wronged me, I do not think about it. I know that is a blessing from God. I give Him all the thanks for working that miracle in my life. Sometimes the memory does come back later, which is why I say forgiveness is continuous.

It is a daily action that we need to purpose in our heart to do each day, for as many times and for as long as necessary. When you can develop a pattern of forgiveness, there will come a time when you think about the offense, and the pain is no longer associated with the action. When you have to forgive the same person over and over, be encouraged and know that God is working it out. *"Then Peter came to Jesus and asked, 'Lord, how many times shall I forgive my brother when he sins against me? Up to seven times?' Jesus answered, 'I tell you, not seven times, but seventy-seven times.'"* Jesus' answer to Peter in verse 22 would appear to be a lot of forgiveness, and it is. *"'No,' he said. 'Not seven times, but seventy seven times'"* (Matthew 18:21-22). In the literal Greek, seventy-seven can be translated either "seventy-seven" or "seventy times seven." The point is not so much about the literal number, but about what Jesus wants to show us concerning grace operating in the life of a believer when it comes to forgiveness.

I sometimes find myself getting frustrated with people who come to me asking my advice on specific things. I share with them what I believe God's Word is saying concerning their situation. Many times they continue on and make no change after hearing the truth. I have to ask God to forgive me for trying to do His job. It is God that changes people—not me; I am incapable of changing anyone.

Unforgiveness can cause you to be sick physically and mentally. One of the great healing balms of the Holy Spirit is forgiveness. When we harbor unforgiveness, it eats at us from the inside. When we fail to forgive, we are hurting ourselves mostly. We like to think holding the grudge is hurting the other person, but that is usually not the case. I remember spending sleepless nights being so angry with someone who hurt me. I would hold onto the anger and just could not seem to let it go.

Once I fully understood that my forgiveness was dependent on me forgiving others, my life took on new meaning. If the truth be told, we really should thank God for people who do us wrong. God can use these situations to draw us closer to Him. It is our enemies that keep us on our knees. It is the adverse situation that causes us to seek the face of a loving and almighty God in our secret places.

God really does have a strong word on forgiveness. He feels so strongly about forgiveness that He commands us as Christians to forgive. Like most of the things God asks us to do, forgiveness is for our benefit. God knows the toll unforgiveness takes on our lives. He understands the weight of such a burden and how it will hinder our purpose. He knows holding unforgiveness in our heart will not allow us to reap the promises of His Word. There are some doors of blessings in our lives that can only be opened by practicing forgiveness. God knows that you and I will never really be healed until we can forgive. We will never really move toward wholeness or be able to get on with our lives until we are able to let go of the resentment and the desire to get revenge. When we can forgive and leave the revenge to God, the process of restoration is working in our lives. *"Do not take revenge, my friends, but leave room for God's wrath, for it is written: 'It is mine to avenge; I will repay,' says the Lord"* (Romans 12:19).

When someone wrongs us, we have to act as God would act. Forgive them not because of who they are but because of who God is. Do not be like me; I pick and chose whom I would forgive and whom I would not forgive. I would base my willingness to forgive or not to forgive on who the offender was, what the deed was, and how likely he or she was to do it again. Well, it is not about me, and it is not about you. It is all about God's grace and His mercy. Even when we do not deserve it, God still shows us His grace and mercy.

So how do you know if you have really forgiven a person or not? If talking or thinking about an event causes you to feel anger, then you have not forgiven the offender. We need God's help to forgive; it is not something we can do on our own. Forgiveness is possible; otherwise, God would not have asked us to do it. He is right beside us helping us to fulfill everything He has asked us to do in His Word.

Forgiveness is a choice; you must decide to forgive. Once you have decided to forgive, God will give you the strength to accomplish the task. Some things you have to "pull" from your memory and leave in the past. The truth is, if you do not forgive others, how can you expect God to forgive you? *"Do not judge and you will not be judged. Do not condemn, and you will not be condemned. Forgive, and you will be for-*

given" (Luke 6:37). When you forgive others, your heavenly Father will forgive you. He will heal and restore whatever hurts you might be experiencing in your life. Friend, you can find the potential of your future because of God's wonderful power operating in your life. Do not let unforgiveness hold you back from your promising future.

God has made forgiving others a requirement for receiving His forgiveness. *"For if you forgive men when they sin against you, your heavenly Father will also forgive you. But if you do not forgive men their sins, your Father will not forgive your sins"* (Matthew 6:14,15). *"Be kind and compassionate to one another, forgiving each other, just as in Christ, God forgave you"* (Ephesians 4:32).

We read so much in the Bible about forgiveness. Forgiveness presents a challenge for many of us. I believe the frequent mention of forgiveness in the Scripture is significant to the fact that God knew we would have difficulty practicing forgiveness.

When someone does us wrong, the Scripture teaches that we should not keep a record of it. *"It [love] is not rude, it is not self seeking, it is not easily angered, keeps no record of wrongs"* (1 Corinthians 13:5). Real love is the way God wants us to love each other. *"He who covers over an offense promotes love, but whoever repeats the matter separates close friends"* (Proverbs 17:9). When we are able to forgive, we are promoting love—God's love. If we seek God's forgiveness, we must forgive others.

One of the blessings of forgiveness is joy. Our lives are more joyous when we can forgive others. Unforgiveness keeps us in bondage. *"Blessed [happy] is he whose transgressions are forgiven, who sins are covered. Blessed [happy] is the man whose sin the Lord does not count against him and in whose spirit is no deceit"* (Psalm 32:1-2).

When we forgive, we make a choice to forget. That is not amnesia but a choice not to dwell on the offense.

Brothers, I do not consider myself yet to have taken hold of it. But one thing I do: forgetting what is behind and straining toward what is ahead, I press on toward the goal to win the prize for which God has called me heavenward in Christ Jesus (Philippians 3:13-14).

Forgiveness is important because if we do not forgive, we become bitter and resentment happens. Harboring unforgiveness in our hearts turns our hearts into playgrounds for the devil. Lack of forgiveness will come back to us, adding sorrow to our lives. People who cannot forgive are miserable, and no one likes to be around a miserable person. Bitterness and anger take so much out of you; you feel empty and have nothing to draw from to help others. Forgiveness is not an option for the believer; it is a requirement. There is no way around it; we must forgive one another.

I believe there is a need in every human soul to be able to give and receive forgiveness. We want to forgive, but sometimes we just do not know how. Jesus mentions forgiveness in the prayer He taught the disciples. *"Forgive us our debts as we also have forgiven our debtors"* (Matthew 6:12). You are asking God to treat you the way you treat the people who wronged you. My, my, my, I am so glad we have a merciful God!

Friends, you can be set free from everything that holds you captive. You do not have to live a life of defeat because of unforgiveness. If you are struggling with holding grudges, ask God to help you to forgive. This is one of my daily prayers. Yes, I still have issues. I am by no means where I desire to be, but thank God I have come far from where I used to be.

I looked good on the outside but wrestled with my own

Unforgiveness

private demons brought on by harboring unforgiveness in my heart. If God can change my hard heart and cause me to forgive others, He can do the same for you. Our God is able to help you accomplish your goal. You can forgive others in a way that is pleasing to God. When you forgive someone, you are not allowed to bring action against that person.

You must forgive and leave the person and the offense committed in the hands of a sovereign God. When your forgiveness is genuine, you do not need to tell the person, "I forgive you." When you feel the need to tell them they are forgiven, you have to ask yourself, "Why is that so important to me? Do I need to feel like the better or bigger person?"

Please do not waste years as I did holding onto things everyone else had forgotten. You are only holding yourself back from reaping the promises of God's Word. I express to you today the same words God spoke to me: God wants to put so much more in your hand. Open your heart and let forgiveness flow out, and open your hands and let the promises flow in. When you no longer wish to get even, you will know you are on the way to leaving anger behind and moving forward to receive every promise God has for you in His Word. Friend, I do not want you to miss out on anything God has for you. His Word is filled with promises.

Prayer

Dear Heavenly Father, I pray today that you would place in my heart a deep desire to forgive those who have hurt me. I seek to do Your will and to walk in Your purpose for my life. I know your Word commands that I forgive, but I am unable to do this on my own. I have tried within myself to forgive _____. Just when I think I have forgiven, it comes up again. I truly desire to be obedient, but I confess I need the help of a loving Father to teach me how to forgive.

Seven Blessing Blockers

Father, I ask that just as you have forgiven me, that my heart would be open to forgive others. I refuse to let unforgiveness stand between me and the promises You have for me. I know, according to Your Word, that if I do not forgive those who trespass against me, then You will not forgive me. In Jesus' name, I pray. Amen.

Chapter 4

Attitude

Life is really not that bad, is it? When we look at the large picture, it really could be a lot worse. The truth is, life is more about our attitudes than what actually happens to us. When things go bad for you, what is your attitude? Your attitude can block the flow of God's promises in your life.

I remember voicing my frustrations to God concerning some disappointments I experienced in my life. Of course, He already knew how I felt, so what was the harm in my telling Him? God quickly reminded me that I held certain keys to my future and that my attitude about life would make the difference. That, my dear friend, was a nugget I would have to revisit over and over again. Some years later, I finally understood what God was saying to me: my attitude was the key to my breakthrough.

Job suffered; he lost everything he had, but Job looked up. He kept declaring the favor of God. *"Thou hast granted me life and favor, and thy visitation hath preserved my spirit"* (Job 10:12 KJV). We must remain in an attitude of favor and faith when things are not going according to our plan. Even when your situation has changed, you have to remember God never changes.

The Bible is filled with countless stories of those who kept the right attitude and obtained God's favor. Ruth is one of my favorite women in the Bible, and I encourage you to read this book of the Bible. After losing her husband, Ruth made a decision to follow Naomi to Bethlehem even though it held no promises for her. Ruth's attitude was not one of bitterness or negativity, even when she was surrounded by bitter Naomi. Ruth was rewarded because of her faithfulness to serve her mother-in-law. God blessed Ruth and provided for her. She walked in God's divine favor. Her story is proof that God can restore everything you have lost when you keep the right attitude.

You may be praying and wondering, "Lord when am I going to meet my husband?" Check your attitude; a negative attitude might be your blessing blocker. Ruth was enthusiastic; she did not give up. Each of us must be willing to follow God's lead. Be a woman who is steadfast, a woman with a purpose. Ruth was such a woman; she forsook all and took Naomi's God as her God. God can use you to do extraordinary things when you are completely sold out to Him.

I declare the favor of God over my life and the life of my family every day. I pray with my children before they go to school. I declare God's favor over their lives as they interact with teachers, staff, and other students. God's favor can do for you what you could never accomplish on your own. When negative things happen, do not adopt a negative attitude. If people around you are talking negative and you feel yourself being pulled in, ask to be excused. This is the one time I give my children permission to run away.

In our family, we teach our children the power of their words.

Attitude

I tell you the truth, if anyone says to this mountain, Go throw yourself into the sea, and does not doubt in his heart but believes that what he says will happen, it will be done for him. Therefore I tell you, whatever you ask for in prayer, believe that you have received it, and it will be yours (Mark 11:23-24).

Our daughter Jade wanted to be a part of the show choir at her middle school. She was a new student at the middle school in eighth grade. She had been involved in chorus in her former school but never in the public school system. When I inquired about her becoming a part of the show choir, I was told that those students were selected the previous year. In order to qualify, Jade should have been a chorus student for two years with this particular chorus teacher. When I told Jade, she responded, "I am going to take my audition tape to school and ask the chorus teacher, 'When can I audition?'" not 'Can I audition' but "When can I." Notice the difference. Needless to say, Jade was in the show choir that year and sang several solos.

She understood the principle of speaking positively. She also understood the principle of ask and you shall receive. *"Ask and it will be given to you"* (Matthew 7:7). *"You may ask me for anything in my name, and I will do it"* (John 14:14). She knew enough to know that she needed to ask and not just take no for an answer.

You want something but don't get it. You kill and covet, but you cannot have what you want. You quarrel and fight. You do not have, because you do not ask God. When you ask, you do not receive, because you ask with wrong motives, that you may spend what you get on your pleasures (James 4:2-3).

The Scripture teaches that many times we do not receive simply because we do not ask.

Obtaining the favor of God sounds easy, but there are conditions.

Dear friends, if our hearts do not condemn us, we have confidence before God and receive from him anything we ask because we obey his commands and do what pleases him (1 John 3:21-22).

It goes back to your relationship with God. Are you in a covenant relationship with Him?

Attitude plays such an important role in our lives on a daily basis. I find that when I have a positive attitude, my experiences are more favorable than when I have a negative attitude. While recently attending my family reunion in North Carolina, we encountered several favorable experiences at our hotel. Our room was the first room on the first floor as you come in the side door. Now that might have seemed negative for some, but we were thrilled. It meant a shorter walk with our luggage and easy access to the car if we forgot something. We were also able to get what we considered to be the perfect parking space—the end space only a few steps from the side door of the hotel.

The next morning when the girls and I drove to the mall, I thought, "Well, there goes my perfect parking space." I immediately stopped myself before the words could come out of my mouth. That is what you have to do when negative thoughts come in your mind—stop them and replace them with God thoughts. I starting thinking, "favor, favor, favor." When we got back a few hours later, the space was still free. Keep the right attitude, and you can walk in favor all day.

Later that day we went out to an afternoon event, and we were gone for about five hours. By the time we returned, that parking space was gone, but God provided a better one. There was an empty parking space on the end, right in front of the

Attitude

side door. This was especially nice when we started to load the car the next morning at 6:00 a.m.

Now I know you might be thinking, "Parking spaces, what is the big deal?" Have you ever been to Wal-Mart and tried to get an up-close parking space in the afternoon? I have. I went to Wal-Mart in the middle of the afternoon crowd. While I was driving around the parking lot, I started declaring God's favor. I got the first parallel parking space in front of the doors. I had never been in that space before, not even at 7:30 in the morning, which is when I usually go to Wal-Mart.

The next time I went to Wal-Mart I thought, *Well let's try this again.* It was about the same time of day, and I got the same space again. Minutes after we got in the store, it began to pour down rain. You would have thought the roof was coming down on the building. One thing you can always count on in Tampa during the rainy season is a storm every afternoon around 4:00 p.m. I told the girls, "This is great. At least when we come out, we will not have to walk far in the rain." Much to my pleasure, by the time I gathered my items and started to my nearby parking space, the rain had ceased. Another thing about Tampa is the daily downpour of rain does not last long.

As most of you know, this is not always the outcome in a Wal-Mart parking lot, but the key is to keep the right attitude. If you keep a positive attitude, then even when you are unable to locate a good parking space, it will not change your outlook for the day.

Your attitude is the key to you getting victory over your circumstances. Do not allow things, people, or situations to cause you to be negative. You have to learn to see a bright side to everything that happens in life. Sometimes it is difficult to see the silver lining because it is being blocked by the clouds.

When I get up in the morning, I expect to have a great day. Even if I have disappointments during the course of my day, it has still been a great day. I am so excited about what tomorrow holds that sometimes it is hard for me to live in the present. A few years ago, my story was very different. I worried so much about tomorrow that I could not enjoy the present. Today I live in the other extreme; I can hardly wait to see what tomorrow holds. I expect God's favor every day.

I remember when I had a little accident with my then two-month-old car. The damage was minor, but I wanted to have it repaired. I did not know any local mechanics in the area, so I made an appointment to take the car to the dealer. Of course, everybody knows going to the dealer with a small repair like that is not a wise choice.

People were telling me, "I would not go to the dealer for something like that; they will charge you $50 or $60 just to look at it." I went to the dealership *expecting* favor. The service advisor quoted me $140 to fix the problem.

As I sat in the waiting room, I begin to write my prayers for that day in my prayer journal. One of my prayers said, "God I am expecting your favor even in this situation." It took about ten minutes, and the service advisor came to me and said, "Mrs. Taylor, I have good news. The technician I assigned to your car had everything you needed in his bay. He asked me not to charge you, so I am just going to void this ticket." They brought my car around and as I walked out the door, he handed me a yellow rose and said, "Please accept this from us." By this time, my daughters were looking at me with that "what is going on" face. I looked at them and shouted the words they hear often from my mouth, "Favor, favor, favor!"

I could tell you countless incidences where God's favor showed up in my life. The key is to have an attitude of expectance. Always expect God's favor, and do not look at your

Attitude

situation. Do not rely on what you feel, but choose to believe what God's Word says about you. Choose to expect His favor everyday and in every circumstance. Somebody said, "What if I do not get the favor I am expecting?" I would rather expect it and not get it than not to expect it at all.

A good attitude can bring much success in life; a bad attitude can bring destruction. Negative attitudes are just as contagious as positive attitudes. Our attitudes result from our perception. Our perceptions are our observations or awareness of our environment. Our perceptions of our lives can be affected by many things, including our past. Sometimes we rely on others to form our perceptions. We need to learn how to look beyond our perceptions and change our attitudes.

Most of the troubles in our lives are caused by our attitudes. Check your attitude and pray for deliverance from negative attitudes. Your attitudes affect every part of your life. You also affect others around you by your attitude.

When you are going through a trial, instead of asking, "Why am I going through this?" ask, "Why am I still here? Why didn't this challenge destroy me?" There is a purpose for everything you go through in your life. If the enemy had known that in the face of adversity you would pray more, he would have never messed with you. If satan had known attacking you in this way would drive you to seek a closer walk with God, he would have left you alone.

Living a life of purpose is critical to your good health. When you are living a life of purpose, your positive attitude can save your from the stress, heartburn, headaches, and all the other physical symptoms that a negative attitude will present in your body. I have learned that even when I have sickness in my body, if I can keep the right attitude, the discomfort does not last as long. When I complain about how bad I feel, that's when my distress lingers.

We sometimes allow ourselves to get so frustrated because we want to know everything now. We want every answer now. We need to believe God has a plan, even if we do not know what it is. Know that His plan is good.

Finally, brothers, whatever is true, whatever is noble, whatever is right, whatever is pure, whatever is lovely, whatever is admirable—if anything is excellent or praiseworthy—think about such things. Whatever you have learned or received or heard from me, or seen in me—put it into practice. And the God of peace will be with you (Philippians 4:8-9).

Paul is giving us the remedy for negative thinking. He is telling us what we should be thinking about.

If you believe in the goodness of God and want God's approval, then you should fix your mind on things that are holy and right. Think about things that are pure and beautiful. Our conduct should model the teachings of Paul in this Scripture. Think on good things because God is good.

Bad may be happening all around us, but God is still good. Sometimes circumstances may not seem to be good, but remember God cares about you. Put a smile on your face and a song in your heart. God loves you always, and He has not forgotten you.

I like to use the model of a person believing God for healing. Even if I die with the disease, I would rather die believing that God will heal me than to die not believing. God is faithful to perform His Word. I do not know why or how He decides to do what He does, but one thing I know for sure is that God is faithful.

There are times in my life that I sit down to think with the intention of focusing on the negative. I am immediately convicted, and I begin to give thanks to God. Life is not always easy, but God is still good. Even when life seems bad, God is still good. The challenges of your day may have been horrible, but that does not diminish God in any way. He is still God, and He is still good.

I have not always expected favor in my life. Yes, in some areas, I expected favor while in others I expected failure. It is not a surprise to me now to know that the areas in which I expected failure were the areas in which I failed.

We have to change the way we think. God's favor is free to everyone who believes. God does not have favorites. "There is neither Jew nor Greek, slave nor free, male nor female, for you are all one in Christ Jesus" (Galatians 3:28).

Our attitudes can bless others or cause others to avoid us. It is more about how we speak the truth and less about what we speak. No one likes to be reprimanded, but if we must reprimand, we need to do so with the right attitude. It will be received better.

Do not let what others do or say affect your attitude. We have to be careful what we receive. Any mood or attitude satan offers needs to be resisted and not received. The enemy can plug into us and violate us through his subtle tactics, and that is why it is so important that we keep our focus on the promise. The present state may look bleak and the future not much better from our eyes, but we must focus on what has been consistent. Focus on what never changes. God never changes; He will not violate His Word. Instead of complaining, start praising God and thanking Him for His bountiful blessings. *"Your attitude should be the same as that of Christ Jesus"* (Philippians 2:5).

What does God's Word say about it? That is the question to ask yourself when you are feeling down. The situation may look hopeless, but it is not the end. It is about choices; choose to believe what God has said. If God said it, then it is settled, even when your friends tell you, "It will not happen, and you might as well give up." What did God say? When everything around you is negative, what did God say? Search the Scriptures to see what God has said about your situation. Make the choice to believe what God has said, even when it looks like everything is against you. Make the decision not to let anyone or anything determine your attitude on any given day. It is about choices; we have the ability to choose to believe God.

Prayer

Dear Father, I pray today for the right attitude. I pray that You would help me to choose a positive attitude in every area of my life. Even when things are not going as I have planned them, help me to trust You. I know You have a plan for me, and I choose to believe Your Word. I declare Your favor over my life today and every day. I declare Your favor over my family and every person to whom I am connected. If I have any ungodly connections, I pray that they are broken now in the name of Jesus. Father, let my attitude reflect that of a loving God. Let me always display an attitude that will point others to You. As I go today, I will expect Your favor, and the anticipation of Your favor will be displayed in my attitude. Thank you, Father, for Your favor in my life always. In Jesus' name I pray. Amen.

Chapter 5

Pride

Have you ever thought you knew something, only to find out you did not? When we rely on our own abilities and neglect to consult God, we are setting ourselves up for a fall. God created us to have fellowship with Him. He wants to be involved in our daily lives. When we seek to follow our own agenda without regards to what He has said, we are being prideful.

Pride will hold you back from where God wants to take you. Often we go through life thinking, *I can do this*. Often we think of ourselves as being self-sustaining and say, "I can do this all by myself." We think we can make it without help from others and that we are strong enough on our own. In order for the promises of God to be manifested in our lives, one very important discovery must be made.

We must realize and accept that without God not only can we do nothing but without God, we are nothing. We are weak; it is God who is strong. It is He who helps us through the tough times in our lives. As God sustains us, we must point others to the almighty God. He is a very present help in times of trouble. When others are confused, we can avail ourselves to talk and to pray with them, but ultimately it is God who heals the broken.

In Scripture we read, *"Each one should test his own actions. Then he can take pride in himself, without comparing himself to somebody else"* (Galatians 6:4). Paul is teaching us that anyone who concludes that he is something special when comparing himself to those who have fallen is fooling himself. As believers, we have no room to judge others; we must examine ourselves and make certain that our relationship with the Father is correct.

According to *Webster's Dictionary*, pride is "the quality or state of being proud as inordinate self-esteem: conceit." Pride also refers to having a reasonable amount of justifiable self-respect. For the purpose of what I want to share with you in this book, we will be discussing the negative pride that one can possess, as in a haughty or arrogant person. This, my friend, is the form of pride that stands between you and the promises of God.

In my daily Bible reading, I was reminded just how much pride displeases God. Although I had read through the Bible before, I did not recall this one particular Scripture:

Instantly, an angel of the Lord struck Herod with a sickness, because he accepted the people's worship instead of giving the glory to God. So he was consumed with worms and died (Acts 12:23 NLT).

When we allow pride to dwell in us, we take on a form that was never meant for man. God is the one to be highly exalted, not you and certainly not me. God will not share His glory with us; the glory belongs solely to Him. That is why the Lord's Prayer says, "Thine is the kingdom, the power and the glory." Pride is a setup for a letdown; please do not get caught in that trap.

Pride

My husband has openly confessed that he has struggled with pride in his life. Although if you met him now, you would never think pride was an issue for him. All the glory and honor goes to God for transforming my husband's life. God can do the same for you and for anyone who trusts Him. When we think more highly of ourselves than we should, we are treading on dangerous ground.

It is easy to identify characteristics in others that we consider prideful. The mirror of God's Word wants each of us to look at ourselves. We have to look inward to see what is holding us back. Seeing everyone else's faults and not your own is a sign that pride could be blinding your eyes.

I have always had high expectations of myself, and I expected equally as much from others. My husband, who was raised very different from me, tends to give others the benefit of the doubt. I have learned so much from watching how he accepts people and how he gives them an opportunity to grow.

I was raised in a very strict Christian home. There were many activities we were not allowed to do. It was not until later, through my studying and understanding of God's Word, that I realized I could have fun and not be sinning. I do not fault my parents for having high standards. I am sure it is because of their example I am who I am today. I do understand now, though, that not everyone had the same firm teaching I had growing up. This helps me to allow others to be themselves and still love them.

It is God who changes the hearts of people, and it is not my place or anyone else's place to stand in judgment. Do not let a prideful heart make you look at others with contempt. The Bible teaches, *"all have sinned and fall short of the glory of God"* (Romans 3:23).

Here are a few Scriptures that will show us how God regards pride—He hates it:

To fear the Lord is to hate evil; I hate pride and arrogance, evil behavior and perverse speech (Proverbs 8:13).

Pride can cause us to fall into sin; for this reason, we must hate pride just as God hates it. Pray for an eye to discern evil and the wisdom to avoid it.

When pride comes, then comes disgrace, but with humility comes wisdom (Proverbs 11:2).

Pride goes before destruction a haughty spirit before a fall (Proverbs 16:18).

A man's pride brings him low, but a man of lowly spirit gains honor (Proverbs 29:23).

God lifts the humble person and puts down the prideful person.

You rebuke the arrogant, who are cursed and who stray from your commands (Psalm 119:21).

This next verse refers to a person desiring the office of a Bishop or Overseer. *"He must not be a recent convert, or he may become conceited and fall under the same judgment as the devil"* (I Timothy 3:6).

For everything in the world, the cravings of sinful man, the lust of his eyes and the boasting of what he has, and does comes not from the Father but from the world (I (John 2:16).

When we become lifted in pride, we are prey for the devil. We become conceited and fall into the trap of becoming judgmental and critical of others. If you recognize something in another person that you believe will hinder their destiny, pray about it and ask God to show it to them. It is not your place to be the Holy Spirit in another person's life. If God directs you, go to them in humility.

Pride

I know as wives that we like to point out our husbands' faults. We sometimes feel it is our duty to point out their shortcomings. We think, *If I do not tell him, who will?* That is God's job, not ours. Praying is always more effective than pointing; let God make any necessary changes.

Remember, God looks at your heart. Pride is more about the heart and less about appearances. It has to be all about God and not about us—make God a priority. The moment it becomes about me, God is not in it. It is not what we have, but how we feel about what we have. God can bless us abundantly, but we must remain humble so He can use us.

I know many proud, boastful people who have very little. On the other hand, I know others who possess great wealth but yet remain quite humble and seem to enjoy life's most simple pleasures.

I worked as a real estate agent for five years in Maryland. Realtors always seem to drive expensive cars, at least the "successful" ones. I remember sharing with a fellow agent in my office one day about the true meaning of success. She thought driving the nicest car was the definition of success. What you have parked in your driveway is not God's definition of your success. There is nothing wrong with driving a nice car, but God never chooses us because of what we have, what we drive, or for any of the reasons we deem as successful.

God chooses us because of what we do not have. God wants to take what we consider to be failures and do a work in our lives. He wants to make a transformation for which only He can take the credit. If we could do it ourselves, we would not need God. All the glory belongs to Him for any measure of success we have achieved in life or will achieve.

We cannot do anything without God. We would not have anything without Him. It is all about Him. Even our struggles are about Him and what He wants to do in our lives. Our salvation is about Him. Our marriage is about Him. Every good work we do is about Him, or it should be about Him. God has no ego, so why should we? Without Him, we cannot accomplish anything. He is all powerful and we are not. He is all knowing and we are not. Let go and let God. He desires to do great and marvelous things in our lives.

The Lord is my light and my salvation whom shall I fear? The Lord is the stronghold of my life of whom shall I be afraid? (Psalm 27:1).

God is our refuge and strength (Psalm 46:1).

I can do everything through Him, who gives me strength (Philippians 4:13).

In my daily prayer I say, "God search my heart. If you find anything contrary to Your Word, please remove it from my heart." There are many times when I want to go my own way and do my own thing, but I am convinced that to walk in my own way blocks God's blessings in my life. I desire His blessing more than I desire to be right. I desire His favor more than I want to get my own way and do my own thing. Getting one's own way is short-term gratification; I prefer God's blessing forever.

Do not let pride stand in the way of you fulfilling your destiny. You must submit your will to God. When He is in control of your life, He will reveal to you His will for your life. God can cause your dreams to become a reality. He is all-powerful. Do not try to work things out with your own power, but trust God. Remember that what you birth in the flesh, you must maintain in the flesh. When you submit to God and allow Him full control, it will liberate you. It is freeing to know that I am not alone in this fight and that I do not have to do it by myself.

Pride

I have submitted my will and my way to God, and I continue to do so daily. In my prayers each day, I commit my life to Him again. I know you might wonder if that is necessary. For me it is, because many days before I even leave my house I realize I have put my will before His will. It is a daily process to stay focused on what God wants me to do and be less focused on what I want to do.

Pride will not allow us to show others our true selves. In my circle, I was always the strong one, and everyone looked up to me. I had an image to maintain my position, so there was no way people could know what I was really feeling. I was not about to tell them or show them. I was never really good at verbalizing my feelings, which was my excuse for not sharing my vulnerabilities with others.

Friends, it is only when we become broken before God that we can be used by God. In our brokenness, He will show us how to deal with our false image. I have experienced many frustrations in my life, most of which I kept bottled up inside of me. I felt as if I had no one to go to who would understand. I did not want other people to see me as weak. Finally, my body began to show physical symptoms of a person who was stressed, even though to the onlookers I appeared calm. If only they could see inside me, they would be surprised. Keeping up a facade like that all the time is no easy task.

When I began to focus more on God and the awesome power of who He really is, my life began to change. I started to focus less on my abilities and even less on my inabilities. I came to the conclusion that the universe did not revolve around me. It could not be about how I felt, what I wanted to do, or what I thought I needed to say. I allowed God to take control, and my prideful heart began to break free of the bonds that held me. I began to experience a new life in Christ Jesus, a free and open life.

Pride will cause you to avoid taking responsibility for your actions. You do not want to appear as someone who has failed or one who has made a mistake. It is easier to blame someone else rather than admit your own shortcomings. Pride will blind you to the truth concerning who you really are. You begin to live a lie based on what you want others to perceive about you.

God is looking for someone with a heart for Him, a woman who is available for whatever God needs her to do. He wants a woman who is willing to serve and to build up the kingdom of God here on earth. When you are a woman seeking the heart of God, then you are a woman that can be used by God. God desires humble servants. He is seeking those who have no hidden agenda but a willingness to obey. When Jesus called His disciples, He called them to service. In order to lead others, we must first be His servants. God wants those who are willing to endure challenges like a good soldier, and He will bring them victory.

As believers, we must put into daily practice the fruit of the spirit. Our lives should display these characteristics. *"But the fruit of the Spirit is love, joy, peace, patience, kindness, goodness, faithfulness, gentleness, and self-control. Against such things there is no law"* (Galatians 5:22-23). When others look at us, let them see these attributes demonstrated in our lives. The fruit of the spirit should be plentiful in our lives and include no shortages.

We must represent Christ and His love for mankind everywhere we go and in all we do; after all, we are His ambassadors. *"We are therefore Christ's ambassadors, as though God were making his appeal through us. We implore you on Christ's behalf: Be reconciled to God"* (2 Corinthians 5:20).

Even with our shortcomings, if we are willing and obedient, God can use us to accomplish His purpose for our lives.

We must not allow pride to lift us above where God has called us. When we really think of God's calling on our lives, we realize it has so little to do with what we want to do and more to do with His purpose for us. We are simply the vehicle to be used by God to accomplish the job.

Pride is a pothole created to distract us from the real purpose. When we start to look at ourselves and take our eyes off God, we are destined to fail. We have to take captive our thoughts of selfishness and pride. *"We demolish arguments and every pretension that sets itself up against the knowledge of God, and we take captive every thought to make it obedient to Christ"* (2 Corinthians 10:5).

Pride will hinder us from seeing the truth of who God really is. When we come together for corporate worship, pride can cause us to want to avoid wholehearted worship of God in the presence of others.

> *Yet a time is coming and has now come when the true worshipers will worship the Father in spirit and truth, for they are the kind of worshipers the Father seeks* (John 4:23).

As you lift your hands to acknowledge the awesomeness of God, your heart melts in reverence to Him; it has now become more about God and less about you. Your prideful spirit has been broken through worship.

One of the reasons I am so passionate about worship is because it was only after the pride was gone that I was able to experience true worship. When we worship, we are acknowledging that there is someone bigger and better than we are.

I am not worthy of any great thing, but He is worthy of my worship. We cannot be prideful and be worshippers; the two will not work well together. We must humble ourselves in the sight of God.

In order to love the way God's Word commands us to love, pride must go. If you are dealing with pride, ask God to help you. Confess with your mouth right now that you have a prideful spirit reigning in your heart. Ask God to forgive you and help you to overcome those hindrances. God desires to show you His plan for your life, but you will only see it once the pride is gone. Pride will block your ability to see what God really has for you.

You never want to make another person feel inferior to you, for that is not God's way. He loves each of us and wants only the best for us. Pride can blind your eyes to the truth. If you are prideful, you will only see your needs and overlook the needs of others. To be used by God, you have to be able to discern the needs of other people. If you truly desire to grab hold of the promises of God, you must have a heart free of pride. No one benefits from pride, not even the prideful person.

Never look at another to desire their position. Remember it's not about the position, but it is about the mission. Whatever God has called you to do, He has already made provisions for you to accomplish the task. Please, do not try and duplicate someone else. Be the best you that you can be.

> *Now, brothers, I have applied these things to myself and Apollos for your benefit, so that you may learn from us the meaning of the saying, "Do not go beyond what is written." Then you will not take pride in one man over against another* (1 Corinthians 4:6).

We need to always remember that with God we can accomplish the task. We can always depend on Him; it is when we start to depend on our own abilities and the abilities of others that we fall. My prayer for you today is that you confess any pride that you may have knowingly and unknowingly. God can deliver you today.

Prayer

Dear Heavenly Father, I come to you today confessing the pride that is in my heart. I ask now that You would remove any pride that hinders me from fulfilling Your call in my life. Please search my heart. If You find anything that should not be present in my heart, I pray now that You would remove it. I desire to walk in obedience to Your Word in every area of my life. I want to demonstrate Your love in every way in my life. I pray that You will help me to see others as You see them. Help me not to be judgmental or critical of people but to reach out to them in kindness and love. Lord, I pray for a heart to be more like Yours in every way. When I walk, I want people to see You and not me everyday. I acknowledge my shortcomings. I know I have not been obedient; I have failed to listen when You told me to _____. I felt like I could do it myself. I now confess that I was wrong. I desire to obey You. Please, forgive me and help me to live a life that will point others to You. I denounce the spirit of pride; it will reside no longer in my heart. In Jesus' name I pray. Amen.

Chapter 6

Fear

"For God gave us not a spirit of fearfulness; but of power and love and discipline" (2 Timothy 1:7 ASV)

God's spirit does not teach fear or weakness but power, love, and self control. When we are in covenant agreement with God and fulfilling His commandments, we do not have to be afraid. Whatever we need, God can supply. There is nothing too difficult for Him. What may seem impossible for man to accomplish is an opportunity for God to work a miracle.

Many years ago I received my first official "women's ministry" assignment. A young woman who had been in an abusive marriage for about four years came to me. She asked if I would mentor her. She needed some help getting past all the anger from the abusive relationship in which she had been involved. She wondered if she would ever have a healthy relationship. I immediately gave her all my excuses as to why I was not the person to mentor her. I made excuses and told her, "I do not have the time, and I am not qualified."

The young woman began to share with me about how she had been blessed by watching my life. She told me she had watched my growth over the past few years and how much she admired my love for God. I told her to let me pray about it, which is the "Christian answer" (you know, the answer we give when we really would rather not do something). Fear was the real reason I felt I could not help her.

When I prayed, God began to show me that I was just an instrument that He could use to bring forth change. If I were unwilling to participate, He could just as easily use somebody else. If I truly meant what I said when God called me to minister to women, then I must allow God to use me. I had told God, "I am available to be used by You." Now it was time to put my words into action. What I had to understand was that the Holy Spirit had given me a spiritual gift, and the Holy Spirit would empower me to use the gift. I begin to meet with this young woman on a weekly basis. God really blessed our time together. With the help of God, she was able to escape the hurt of her past.

She is now happily married to a man who loves God and loves her. She was able to resolve the anger and move into the promise of God for her life. I had to understand that it was God who would bring the necessary healing in her life and that I was to trust in Him, not in my own ability.

You cannot allow fear to rule your life. The Holy Spirit will give you power for the various situations of ministry. God wants us to trust Him with every area of our lives. The love the Holy Spirit gives us should be directed toward others. We have to use our gift to help others.

When I left Maryland in 1990, I was headed to North Carolina. I was going to help my mother take care of my father. He had been diagnosed with cancer a few years prior. In addition to the cancer, he had recently suffered a stroke and was no long able to care for himself. My mother was unable to do the required lifting without assistance. Our family agreed not to put him in a facility.

With my nursing degree and twelve years experience, I had both the knowledge and the skill to care for him at home. I was more than qualified, and I was also willing to help my mother care for him.

I left a career on Capitol Hill that I loved, sold my home, and left my friends. At the time, I was actively seeking a mate and trusting God for marriage. I was told by others, "If you want to meet someone, why are you going to the country?" My parents lived about ten miles from the nearest town. Believe me when I tell you, if I was to meet my husband, God would have to orchestrate it.

Fear could have kept me in the big city, but faith took me to the country. I was there for about a week when I received a telephone call from a young man who introduced himself as Scott Taylor. I thought to myself, *God, the last thing I am thinking about now is meeting someone. Why now?* This was not a good time for me to begin a relationship. Again, fear was at work and telling me, "This is not the time for this, so forget it."

God's plan is always best. We talked on the telephone that night for over an hour, and we prayed at the end of the conversation. He called me back the next day and the next. After a few weeks of conversation and prayer on the telephone, never having met face to face, he asked me to marry him. I said, "Yes." We both believed that was the plan of God for our lives. God is faithful to fulfill His Word when we trust Him. I was on the backside of nowhere, and God had sent me my husband. No wonder the Bible said, *"He who finds a wife finds what is good and receives favor from the Lord"* (Proverbs 18:22). Scott certainly had to find me in Bladen County, North Carolina.

I met him for the first time about four weeks later, and he got down on one knee with the diamond ring in hand and proposed to me (again). Friends, you cannot allow fear to control your lives. Scott was in Maryland where I had been for eight years. Ironically, he had been there for eight years also, but we did not know each other existed. It was when I stopped operating in fear and followed the plan of God for my life that I received what I so desperately wanted. Do not worry about missing out. God knows where you are. The blessings of the Lord will overtake you. *"All these blessings will come upon you and accompany you if you obey the Lord your God"* (Deuteronomy 28:2). You do not have to seek the blessing. Seek the Lord who blesses, and the blessing will find you.

Continue to obey God always, and He will not disappoint you. Close your ears to what satan has to say, and open your heart to what God is saying. The enemy will use people to speak fear into your life, but do not receive it. People would tell me, "What are you waiting on? You better not let that one get away. Maybe you missed your husband." People who should have been speaking life into me and encouraging me were speaking words of death to me. I thank God for the heart He gave me to please Him. I want to encourage you never to give up on God. He is working on your behalf all the time. Do not let your fears cause you to lose faith, for God is on your side. As long as God is on your side, you do not have to fear what men say or do. I am so glad I did not settle but waited on God.

I was a dedicated runner; I would run five to six miles every day, weather permitting. I was pleasantly surprised when Scott told me he was a runner also and how much he enjoyed being outdoors. I told him how I would run, look at the sky, and thank God for the man He had for me. I would say, "God, I know out there in this big world that the man you have for me is looking at this same sky praying for me." Scott told me he used to run and pray the same prayer for the woman God had for him. Friends, I know you have heard this before, but I want to express it again, "Wait on the Lord!" Please do not get in a rush to be married; God has your mate. When you can trust God, He will fulfill every desire of your heart in His own time. The Scripture says, *"But seek first his kingdom and his righteousness, and all these things will be given to you as well"* (Matthew 6:33). Walk uprightly before God, and I promise He will bless you. *"For the Lord God is a sun and shield; the Lord bestows favor and honor; no good thing does he withhold from those whose walk is blameless"* (Psalm 84:11).

Fear will hold you back from where God wants to take you. God may be calling you to a ministry, and you could be letting fear hold you back. One of my greatest fears as a believer was not fulfilling the call of God on my life. I worried I would return to my heavenly Father having not done what He sent me here to do. Through much teaching and a better understanding of God's Word, I learned that as long as I am obedient and follow the plan of God for my life, I could not fail. I now understand that I am right on schedule for what God has called me to do. I may be behind schedule or ahead by man's expectations, but I am right where God wants me. I live my life now with no regrets.

Every day when I get up, I get up with a purpose. Some days the purpose is different from what I had planned, but I know I am always where God wants me. I pray daily for Him to order my steps. Often I have a written agenda for my day, and situations will take me off task. The very condition that took me off task was designed by God to position me where He wants me for that time and for His purpose.

When situations arise in my life that would seem to produce fear, I have learned to trust God. When our first child was born, I had some complication that required an immediate Caesarean section. I guess I should have been fearful when they had to give me general anesthesia with a temperature of 105 degrees. My husband tells the story of how he was asked to leave the operating room as they were strapping my arm down. In his state of panic, he said I began to sing "Come Thou Fount." In the midst of all the chaos, God gave me peace. *"He will have no fear of bad news; his heart is steadfast, trusting in the Lord"* (Psalm 112:7).

Many people I meet in the course of a day live with deep-seated fears. Some of these fears date back to their early childhood, and they still struggle with them as adults. Issues that have never been dealt with will always give you trouble. I want to encourage you to seek God and ask Him to show you the areas in your life that will cause you problems later. Allow God to heal you everywhere you hurt.

I have the awesome opportunity to minister to pastors' wives. Many of these precious women live in isolation because of fear. They ask, "Who can I go to about my struggles?" People look up to me. Many of them fear what others will think of them. They are concerned about the repercussions to their husbands' ministries if the truth were revealed. Their greatest need is someone to confide in, someone who will understand. Fear causes them to keep things bottled up inside. They have no one they can trust, no one with whom they can be transparent. They fear that if anyone really knew what went on in their homes that they would not understand. I agree their concerns are in some ways legitimate because some people will not understand. But let me reassure you, my sister, God *does* understand; and we can always go to Him with our fears.

I went through many years in my life seeking someone to talk to about things I did not understand. I remember feeling so alone. I knew God was with me, but I needed to connect with another human. I prayed for God to send me a friend, a real confidant, someone I could be open with, and someone who cared. I see myself in so many of the precious women with whom I am privileged to meet. Their role as first lady will not allow them to be transparent. My dear friend, God cares, and He knows your struggles. He has a confidant prepared just for you—someone you can trust. Have no fear; God is working it out for you right now. Let me encourage you to surround yourself with positive people who can speak into your life. Seek out others who share your role as a pastor's wife and pray about the person with whom you should connect. There will be many who desire to connect to you, but every connection is not a God connection.

We sometimes hold ourselves to a much higher standard than God ever does. Be the person God created you to be. I believe you will like yourself better when you take off the mask. I know I did.

Many times we fear our own success. What if I succeed, then what? I might have to do something I am not comfortable doing. So, in order to get around the fear of success, we do not try. The one sure way not to succeed is not to try.

God wants us to accomplish our dreams. We cannot be afraid to step out on faith and trust God. He has given each person a measure of faith. We have to use our measure to walk toward what we believe the plan of God is for our lives.

When I was writing this book, one of my fears was, "What if the book is a success?" If the book was a success, then people would want me for speaking engagements, and I do not like to fly. Many times we hold ourselves back. We are the leading hindrances in our own lives. We have to be willing to walk through the doors as God opens them.

We sometimes fear what people will think about us. We crave the approval of others, many times even from people we do not like. Our society is so programmed that we need the approval of other people. God is calling us to be individuals. We do not need to try to be like others. Just be yourself.

The Scripture calls us daughters of Sarah (I Peter 3:1-6). We are daughters of Sarah when we are not afraid, when we remain calm and keep control, and when we rebuke fear, trust in God, judge God faithful, and learn to smile through our tears. *"Like Sarah, who obeyed Abraham and called him her master. You are her daughters if you do what is right and do not give way to fear"* (1 Peter 3:6).

One of the fears that held me captive for many years was a fear concerning our finances. Before my husband and I were married, we agreed that I would handle the finances. We decided this because of my love for mathematics and my ability to handle money. I had a good track record as a single woman and had proven my skills at budgeting and saving. My husband, on the other hand, had a shaky record. Although he had a lucrative career, he liked to spend a lot of money.

He had many good qualities (and still does), but handling money back then was not one of them. Maybe he just did not want the headache of handling the money; I am not really sure of his reasons. He had no problem with me doing the finances, and I was more than happy to take care of this.

I felt very confident that I would have no trouble in this area as long as my husband gave me free reign, which he did. So years later when God begin to deal with my heart about my controlling the finances, I was fearful. I thought releasing control meant inevitable poverty for our family. As God begin to speak with me concerning my fears, I realized it was not my husband I did not trust. Ultimately, it is God who provides for us, so my fear was that God would not take care of our family.

I repented and did what I knew God was asking me to do. I felt a little bad for my husband because this was a particularly vulnerable time in our finances. We had just relocated, I was not working, and starting over was presenting some challenges. The most amazing thing happened when my husband began to manage the budget for our family. There was always money left over for the fun things we were never able to do before without going into debt. It was what I describe as a supernatural occurrence. I would go to the grocery store shopping and get the same things I always bought, but at the checkout, the bill would be less.

My frequent trips to the grocery store stopped, and the food I would buy lasted longer than before. When we live in fear, we doubt the truths of God Word. We must overcome fear if we are to reap the promises of God's Word.

You may experience similar fears in your own life. You may have fears of illness, of death, and of raising your children, wondering how they will turn out. There is always something to fear if we allow ourselves to be taken in by it. For as many acts of faith we experience, there are an equal number of fears. Over the years, I have had more fears than faith. I now wonder why it took me so long to grab onto faith and let go of fear.

I went through a period in my life where I suffered from anxiety. I was anxious about everything. My life was filled with "what ifs"; I had to know the end before the beginning. If I could not figure it out, I was frustrated; I worried about everything. One of the things I feared was dying. Every little pain I had would set my mind to racing. I lived in a "what if" state. I would lie in my bed at night and worry sometimes would elevate my blood pressure.

My emotions were out of control; I later learned that some of the emotional turmoil I was experiencing was hormonal. Even in the midst of hormonal imbalances, I still had to trust God to direct me as to the best way to handle the situation.

He is still God, and there is nothing too difficult for Him. *"Ah, Sovereign Lord, you have made the heavens and the earth by your great power and outstretched arm. Nothing is too hard for you"* (Jeremiah 32:17).

I learned to trust God and believe what He said rather than what I thought to be the truth. Once I was able to understand that what I feared was not real, it liberated me. I had to separate what was real from what was "what if." Some of my issues were related to my need to control everything. I needed to be in control of my life, and I needed to know what would happen tomorrow. And because no one knows what will happen tomorrow, not knowing would make me anxious.

Once the Word of God liberated me, I began to walk lighter because I knew the responsibility was no longer mine. God had a plan, and it was His responsibility to perform and to fulfill the plan He had for my life. I understood He did not need my help; it was not my responsibility to fulfill God's plan. After all, it was His plan, and He was perfectly capable of seeing it come to pass.

Life during that time was not much fun at all. I worried about everything and everybody. I could not watch certain things on television without wondering, *What if that happens to me?* If I had an abnormal test or laboratory results, I would immediately think the worst. Perhaps that is why God has put so many people in my life who suffer from anxiety disorders. I speak their language; I know what it feels like to have to carry the burden of life on my shoulder, and I know what it feels like to release it to an almighty God.

Friends, we serve a God who never sleeps. *"Indeed he who watches over Israel will neither slumber nor sleep"* (Psalm 121:4). If He is awake, then you and I can go to sleep. It is not our responsibility to tell the moon when to set or the sun when to rise. It is not within our hands to make something happen or to prevent it from happening. God's Word is true, and every thought that contradicts it is a lie.

Pray and ask God to give you a *rhema* word. A rhema word is a word that God speaks, and the word becomes real to you. When God speaks, His promises are released in your life. In the beginning when God spoke, everything He spoke came out of His mouth. The same God is about to create something in you and through you. The rhema word is the Word of God leaping off the pages of Scripture and releasing a fire of energy inside of you. This kind of creative energy will empower you to act. The power of that Word begins to act in you and through you.

The rhema word is a word that comes by revelation of the Holy Spirit, a life-giving word. As you pray, ask God to make His Word real and alive to you. When God's Word becomes real, you will be able to conquer fear. You will know based on God's Word that fear is not a part of God's plan for you. One spoken Word from God, and your life will never be the same.

Remaining in a constant state of fear will lead to depression. When you are afraid to act, and you allow that fear to hold you back, you feel angry at yourself because fear won. The opposite of fear is faith. When we are fearful and worrying, we are really saying, "God, I do not trust you to take care of this." Once I was able to begin to understand a little about the awesome power of God, I was able to gain some insight from His Word. I understood that nothing would happen in my life of which God was not aware. Not only did He know about it, but He also allowed it. Now I start each day by saying, "Nothing can happen to me today unless God allows it." I know if God allows it, then according to His Word, it's working for my good. *"And we know that in all things God works for the good of those who love him who have been called according to his purpose"* (Romans 8:28).

I like to use the familiar phase, "It's all good." I believe everything that happens in my life ultimately is working for my good. Even when I have a bad experience, some good will result from the experience. It may not seem like it at the time, but I have to believe the Word of God. We must trust God, after all, He is omniscient and He can look in all places at the same time. He sees everything that happens in your life, and nothing is hidden from Him. He is omnipotent and all-powerful; nothing is too difficult for God. He is omnipresent or everywhere. The Psalmist writes about this awesome God who is more than we can ever image.

When we read Psalm 139, we see that God is vigorously searching and testing His servants. He knows everything there is to know about us. The psalm records that He knows when we sit down and when we get up. He knows our motives and our desires.

God knows what we are capable of accomplishing in life. The purpose of all the knowledge God has about us is to protect us. He does not want to use His knowledge against us. He knows our shortcomings, and He is ready to step in where needed to help us fulfill our dreams.

David announces that the work of God in his life dates back to his development in his mother's womb. This helps us to understand that our lives and the meaning of our lives are established from the beginning by God.

When we understand the mighty power of God as it relates to our lives, we can be less fearful. The structures of our lives have been established from the beginning by God. We can trust Him, He will not let us down. When we yield to the design of the Father and allow Him full control of our lives, we have no need to be fearful.

A yielded life of obedience takes away fear. It is only when we begin to trust in our own abilities that we should become fearful. Trusting in oneself is an accident waiting to happen.

David tells us in Psalms 139 that there is no place we can go from the presence of the Lord. Everywhere we go God is there. We cannot hide from an almighty God. The eyes of the Lord are always on us.

I do not know about you, but I am glad He watches over me. The watchful eye of the Lord is not to judge or condemn us but to protect us. He keeps us safe from dangers that we see and from dangers that we do not see.

In our lives, we fear failure, but God's attentive eye is always on us. David desired a world where there was no more evil, no more destruction, no more failures, and no more disappointments. We have to know that no matter what life hands us, God is always ready to deliver us.

There will be times in our life that we will fail. Things will not always turn out the way we desire. We will deal with harsh and ruthless people on this earth. But God is still in control of it all. He is in charge of everything. As long as we trust Him, we will not fail.

I remember reading about Thomas Edison and someone asking him how it felt to have failed so many times trying to invent the light bulb. He indicated that he had not failed but learned many ways that would not work. Anytime we have learned something, that is a success, not a failure. God knows what He is doing in the lives of His children.

God has a plan for your life, and you are the only one who can sabotage it. I now understand that the plan God has for me cannot be derailed by other people. The key to my destiny is wrapped up in my obedience to God.

People close to you will sometimes try to take you off course, but you must stand firmly on God's Word. God knows the plan He has for you; He is the one who devised the plan. The plan God has for you is in His control. It is not left up to circumstances or situations, but God is controlling things. He is carefully navigating and orchestrating the events of your life to bring you to where He wants you to be.

When that revelation of the Word hit my spirit, something happened inside of me: contentment replaced the fear that has previously ruled. God's plan was perfect for me; I did not have to worry about making it happen, that was God's job. All I had to do was obey and follow the plan, and I knew I would succeed. The only way the plan could be hindered was if I walked in disobedience.

The more I began to trust God, the less I worried. In the times we live in now, we have opportunity to fear so much. We are fearful for our children and their safety, and rightfully so. Children are being exploited left and right all over the world. Danger is a frequent visitor to our neighborhoods. Some of the dangers we can identify, but most of the evil plots we are unable to discern without the help of the Holy Spirit. We cannot allow fear to stop us from living our lives; we must learn to trust God. Use wisdom, but leave all the figuring out and processing to God. He is so much better at making things happen than we are.

Do not be fearful of change; most change is good. If you truly desire to do a work for God, flexibility is a must. With a goal to reach the lost, you must be willing to make the necessary changes in order to achieve the goal. Fear will keep you from moving forward. Sometimes you have to put yourself out there and allow God to open the doors that need to be opened and close the ones that need to be closed.

Our fears sometimes are the result of a lack of information. That is why it is so important to ask questions and be informed. Information is power; once you get the answers, you discover the fear was unfounded.

I want to encourage you to be open to the call of God and be willing to be used in whatever capacity to which God calls you. In whatever way God wants to use you, learn to be flexible and willing. God will use us if we make ourselves available for His service. He is looking for willing vessels who will say, "I will go." Put fear out of your life so it will not hold you back.

Fear will tell you that you are not qualified. You do not have to be qualified. God qualifies you when He calls you. Confidence can be cultivated through prayer and reading the Word of God. Reading and listening to positive messages as well as spending time around positive people can also increase your confidence. Know that God has carefully ordered the events of your life to accomplish His plan and purpose in your life. He is moving things, changing things, and pushing you into your promise. Rest in Him, you have to know that He has all things in His control. You can relinquish the reins, because God is in charge. Let Him be God and pray for an ear to hear His voice and a heart to obey His instructions.

Prayer

Dear Heavenly Father, I come to you casting all my fears on You. I know You have not given me the spirit of fear. I release my fears to Your care because I believe You care for me. I refuse to let fear hold me in bondage any longer. I will walk in faith with my head held high. I will not live a life of fear and torment any longer. I refuse to let the enemy cause me to be afraid. I will be obedient to the things that You have called me to do. I will exercise my faith against every obstacle in my life. I proclaim today that I am whole. I am no longer living a life of wishing and hoping. I believe You, and I trust You who created me to perform every promise in my life. If You said it, I receive it. I will not doubt anymore, but I will believe from this day forth. I thank You, Father, for answering my prayer in Jesus' name. Amen.

Chapter 7

Jealousy

Jealousy wants what someone else has, without having to pay the price to get it. It is easy to look at the accomplishments of others and desire them. We do not want to walk the path they took to get to where they are; we just want the end results. Jealousy will cause major problems in our lives.

In Genesis 37-50, we read about the life of Joseph. The story of Joseph and his brothers demonstrates a true picture of the destructiveness of jealousy. Joseph's brothers were so jealous of him that they plotted to get rid of him. Jealousy kept his brothers in the land of Canaan, but their plot to destroy Joseph pushed him into Egypt, which was his place of destiny.

When you allow jealousy to control your actions, you are placing limits on yourself. Your initial goal may be to hurt the other person, but you end up hurting yourself more. Jealousy enters your heart when you resent the goodness of God in the life of another and ignore the goodness of God in your own life. Where jealousy is present, love is absent. *"Love is patient, love is kind. It does not envy, it does not boast, it is not* proud" (1 Corinthians 13:4). If I am jealous, I am envious of another person's blessings and am taking for granted my own blessings.

Many times we are jealous of the material possessions that others may have or of what we think they have. We can be jealous of another person's privileges. When someone has access that we have been denied, sometimes jealousy results. We often become jealous because of the limitations of our own lives and the freedom another might experience in her life. When someone gets promoted and another is overlooked, jealousy is very common in the workplace.

The root of jealousy stems from feelings of inadequacies. Jealousy arises when we do not feel sufficient or worthy. It is the lack of self-esteem that causes us to think that others are better off than we are. When a person does not feel good about herself, it will cause her to look at what others have and desire it. If you struggle with jealousy, you are not alone. Millions of people, especially women, deal with the tendencies to be jealous each day. When you see yourself as a woman of value, you will understand that whatever God gave you is enough to accomplish your dreams. Our self-worth is directly connected to feelings of jealousy, and I will talk in detail about that in chapter eight.

Jealousy is a very negative consuming emotion, and it is impossible to experience true happiness with jealousy in your heart. When you are resentful over what God is doing in another person's life, those selfish feelings steal your joy and leave you feeling miserable and empty. The Scripture says, *"A heart at peace gives life to the body, but envy rots the bones"* (Proverbs 14:30). Jealousy will eat you up on the inside. It is more destructive than cancer. You can become so consumed with monitoring another person's life that you fail to nurture your own life. Jealousy promotes self-pity, and you feel like others are out to get you. If you are not careful, jealousy can lead to blaming God for your shortcomings.

Do not allow your perception of other people to cause jealousy to enter your heart.

Do not fret because of evil men or be envious of those who do wrong; for like the grass they will soon wither, like green plants they will soon die away. Trust in the Lord and do good; dwell in the land and enjoy safe pasture (Psalm 37:1-3).

Be still before the Lord and wait patiently for him; do not fret when men succeed in their ways, when they carry out their wicked schemes (Psalm 37:7).

You can only be the person God created you to be. Being you is the best job for you; no one else can do it as well as you. Many of us are wasting emotional energy being jealous of people for no reason. More often than not, our jealousy is not motivated by a genuine threat. It is usually motivated by a selfish desire to be number one. We crave control and have the need to be better than other people. Does being jealous ever make one's life better? No, it makes one's life worse instead of better.

The Bible is full of examples of the damaging effect of jealousy. We read in Genesis chapter 4 that Cain is jealous of Abel and he kills his brother. The very first murder was caused by jealousy. Cain was a farmer and Abel was a shepherd. Both men worked to bring an offering to the Lord. The offering that Abel brought to the Lord was favorable because God had told them what was an acceptable offering and Abel obeyed. On the other hand, Cain brought what he wanted to bring with no regard for what God had said was acceptable. Cain wanted what Abel had (God's approval), but he did not want to do what Abel did (obey).

God's response to Cain was, "Why are you angry? If you do what your brother did, your sacrifice would have been accepted also." Many times we want the same rewards, but we do not want to pay the same price.

How many times have we seen people wanting to take the short cut and reap the same harvest as a person who sweated in the heat of the day? Have you ever been jealous of someone who has a nice home, never taking into consideration how hard the person works each day?

I have a friend who has worked for more than thirty years in the same field. Now that God has blessed her to be able to afford some luxuries in life, she received a big surprise. The people she thought would be happy and supportive of her were actually jealous of her.

One of the main reasons satan got kicked out of heaven was pride and jealousy. He was jealous of God's power and said, "I want to be God." Jealousy is not of God, it is of the devil. Anytime you feel jealous of another person, know that feeling has originated from the enemy. Negative talk is a sign of jealousy. When you speak negative about others, ask God to search your heart.

Jealousy can cause you to do harmful things and behave in a destructive manner.

> *But the Jews were jealous; so they rounded up some bad characters from the marketplace, formed a mob and started a riot in the city. They rushed to Jason's house in search of Paul and Silas in order to bring them out to the crowd (Acts 17:5).*

Jealousy affects the way we pray. "When Rachel saw that she was not bearing Jacob any children, she became jealous of her sister. So she said to Jacob, Give me children, or I'll die!" (Genesis 30:1). The power of jealousy will cause us to say harsh things. Jealousy consumes your heart in such a way that you will do things or act in ways that are totally out of character for you.

In the story of Joseph, his brothers sold him in order to get rid of him. They meant it for evil, but they did not know they were pushing Joseph into his destiny. God's plan always supersedes the plans of satan.

> *Now therefore be not grieved, nor angry with yourselves, that ye sold me hither: for God did send me before you to preserve life. And God sent me before you to preserve you a posterity in the earth and to save your lives by a great deliverance* (Genesis 45:5,7 KJV).

Joseph's assignment was given by God long before his brother sold him. When we meet opposition, we automatically think it is satan. Quite often, it is God lining up the events of our life to fulfill His purpose. God wants to get us to a place where He can usher us into our next mission. *"Because the patriarchs were jealous of Joseph, they sold him as a slave into Egypt. But God was with him"* (Acts 7:9). I tell you, nothing can happen to you unless God allows it.

I believe today as you read this book that everything the devil did to try and destroy you, God is turning around. Joseph had to experience some things because of the choices his brothers made. He experienced rejection, mistreatment, and he was sold into slavery. In Egypt he was falsely accused, imprisoned, and forgotten. In the end, he was blessed. God turned the situation around. What the enemy used as a means for destruction, God will use to bless you.

When you identify areas in your life where jealousy is prevalent, know that God can remove jealousy and replace it with acceptance and contentment. Just as with any other sin, in order to be forgiven we must confess. Admit that you struggle with jealousy. The Bible teaches, *"But if you harbor bitter envy and selfish ambition in your hearts, do not boast about it or deny the truth"* (James 3:14).

If you want to get rid of the jealousy in your life, you have to come clean before God. Stop denying it. Stop excusing it. Stop justifying it. Stop minimizing it. While jealousy may be petty, it can become a major problem if it is not dealt with properly. God is in control of your life and the lives of the people around you. There is no need to be jealous of others. God sees you and you were uniquely designed by Him.

God is in control of everything, and nothing happens that He does not know about. *"Are not two sparrows sold for a penny? Yet not one of them will fall to the ground apart from the will of your Father"* (Matthew 10:29). Trust God; He knows what He is doing. Do not question His authority. Give Him permission to do what He wants to do in your life. Be grateful for who you are and what you have. Enjoy the blessings that God has already put in your life. Always give thanks for what God has given you. *"Give thanks in all circumstances, for this is God's will for you in Christ Jesus"* (1 Thessalonians 5:18). The more appreciative you become, the less jealous you will be.

Do not look at what other people have but focus on what God has called you to do. Concentrate on accomplishing what you can do for God, and do not worry about others' responsibilities. God's plan for your life cannot be filled by anyone other than you. The grass is not always greener on the other side. I heard someone say, "All grass has to be mowed."

There have been times in my own life where I looked at what someone else had or at what someone else was accomplishing, and I would start to get discouraged and wonder when my day would come. By trusting God and allowing Him to forgive me and strengthen me, I am now able to give thanks in all things. Do not get me wrong, I slip sometimes and fall back into my old habit of looking. But, God is faithful to raise me up to where I should be. We all fall down, but we cannot stay down. We must ask God for help to get back up again. *"For though a righteous man falls seven times, he rises again"* (Proverbs 24:16).

I remember when we were building our home in Maryland. Although I wanted a three-car garage very much, our home had a two-car garage. I was content to live with the decision we had made until construction started on the house next door. Every time I looked out my kitchen window and saw they were getting a three-car garage, I would regret the decision we had made. While I wished our incoming neighbors no ill will and was very happy for them, I wanted a three-car garage too.

One day I verbalized my frustration, showing my lack of appreciation for what we had. That was the day my daughter's third grade class was discussing the tenth of the Ten Commandments. She proceeded to tell the entire third grade class that her mom had disobeyed that commandment. I was a frequent volunteer at the school, and most of the students knew me. In my defense, the teacher told Jade, "Maybe your mom didn't really mean that." Jade said, "No, my mom was not playing. She was serious. She wants the neighbors' house."

> *You shall not covet your neighbor's house. You shall not covet your neighbor's wife, or his manservant or maidservant, his ox or donkey, or anything that belongs to your neighbor* (Exodus 20:17).

I learned a very important lesson that day: we cannot teach our children one thing and let them see us doing another. I also learned that you always have to watch what you say; you never know who is listening.

The definition for jealousy is slightly different than the definition for covet. Both can be equally as destructive. Allowing jealousy or covetousness to enter your heart will destroy you. They are both very negative emotions and are to be resisted at all cost. Jealousy creates anxiety, anger, loneliness, hate, and fear. Your ability to think rationally can be clouded by jealousy. The best counteraction for jealousy is a feeling of security. Be confident in who you are and in whose you are. You have to know that you and everything you have belongs to God. *"For we brought nothing into the world, and we can take nothing out of it"* (1 Timothy 6:7). Friends, remember whatever God has given you is sufficient. When a person feels secure in who they are and in what they have, jealousy can be defeated in her life. If I had been satisfied with our two-car garage home, then I would not have felt the way I did when I saw the neighbors' house being built.

Do not focus on what others are doing but focus on what God is doing. *"The Lord has done this, and it is marvelous in our eyes"* (Psalm 118:23). Give thanks to God for the marvelous things He is doing in your life, and let God deal with others in the way He chooses. Your one focus should be to seek only to please God. When you seek to please others, you are not pleasing God. When you have a sincere desire to please God, your thought process will change. What you once saw as a mountain now looks like a small hill. Maybe nothing has changed in the natural, but because your thought process has changed, your outlook is improved. You no longer see the glass as half empty but half full.

God desires to rid your heart of jealousy. We are commanded to stop all forms of jealousy and envy for our own good. *"Let us not become conceited, provoking and envying each other"* (Galatians 5:26). You do not need to desire what someone else has. Find your contentment, satisfaction, and pleasure in the Lord, not by comparing yourself to others.

Focus on seeking first His kingdom and His righteousness, and you will be less tempted by jealous feelings. What God has for you is so much better for you than what another person may possess. There is no inadequacy in Him. As long as we remain in Him, all of our inadequacies are transformed. With God leading us, we are more than adequate.

Prayer

Heavenly Father, I confess I am jealous of _____.

I have allowed the spirit of envy to come into my heart. Please, Father, forgive me and help me to overcome this obstacle in my life. I know that jealousy does not please You in any way, and it is damaging to my relationship with You. Help me to understand why I am having these feelings and help me to allow You to deal with them in me. Help me to be satisfied with what You have given me. Help me to understand Your grace and to remember always to give thanks. Father, I receive Your forgiveness. I will walk in Your will and purpose for my life. I will not seek to be like anyone else, but I desire to be more like You. In Jesus' name I pray. Amen.

Chapter 8

Self-Image

How many times do we look in a mirror and say, "I do not like what I see"? We may not say it with our mouths, but that is the message we are expressing in our minds. Learning to love ourselves the way God loves us is so important.

You cannot possess the promises of God's Word until you start to see yourself as God sees you. If you do not believe you are whom God says you are, you will always doubt who you really are. You will feel you do not deserve the promises of God. Do not let anyone tell you that you are anything less than who God says you are. My real identity is what God says about me. *"I praise you because I am fearfully and wonderfully made; your works are wonderful, I know that full well"* (Psalm 139:14). The truth is in God's Word.

God created you in His image, and you belong to Him. I refuse to let the enemy make me believe that I am second-class. You do not belong to the enemy; proclaim, "I belong to God." Too many women suffer from low self-esteem. I want you to know how important you are to God. You were not a second thought. You were created with purpose, and there is a

Self-Image

place for you in this world. More importantly, there is a place for you in the body of Christ. I am dedicating my life to teaching and training women and helping them to see their value.

You must build your self-worth on the truth of God's Word. How can you do this? By believing what God's Word says about you. The Bible is full of words of encouragement, which show how God values women. You are important to God in many ways. Women have a special place in the heart of God and in His plan for the world. (Read Romans 16:1-16 and 2 Timothy 1:5.)

Your ability to see yourself as a person of value is directly connected to knowing your purpose. A person without purpose and direction quite often feels insignificant. Without a purpose, you may feel that your contribution to the world does not matter. If you do not know your purpose, then you will not know how to contribute or what to contribute. That is why I believe it is so important to seek God for purpose in our lives. I want you to become purpose focused. When you focus on your *role* in life, and your role changes, then you have an identity crisis. When you focus on your *purpose* for your life, you will have a constant yardstick by which to measure results. You have to measure yourselves by God's standards and not by your own. What does God require of you? Not what others require and not even your own expectations. You need to know if you are meeting God's requirements.

"Then He said to them all if anyone would come after me, he must deny himself and take up his cross daily and follow me" (Luke 9:23). I believe Jesus was saying that we are to deal with whatever life hands us as we go about doing His will. We must learn to lean on Him and trust Him. We have to understand that nothing is more important than following Christ. If we realize God is first in our lives, then we will not worry so much about other things. When we keep our focus

on God and not on what happens in our lives, our self-image/self-worth improves. God wants the best for us; He really does.

In the world, we are measured by what we have. It takes a well-focused, well-grounded person not to lose sight of what is truly important. I believe sometimes God has to awaken us to the simple things in life that we so often take for granted.

Our heart determines who we really are, not our feelings. We should not allow our feelings to dictate how we see ourselves. Even though we may not understand why we feel the way we do, God does. He knows what our feelings are; He can heal us where we hurt.

I can remember being a single woman in my twenties. I had a career, a home, and a nice car, but I just could not seem to meet my Mr. Right. It appeared from the outside that I had it all "going on." I had the latest and most popular hairstyles. I shopped in the upscale department stores. I had the freedom and the finances to travel whenever and wherever I wanted. Meeting eligible bachelors was not a problem for me; I have always been very outgoing and willing to talk to anyone. On any given day, I would meet two or three single men. I had plenty of invitations to go to dinner, movies, or just for a night out. I met and dated nice men and professional men; some were believers, and some were not.

I enjoyed a large circle of good friends, and there was always someone with whom to spend time. I was busy serving my church in many capacities, and I loved God with my whole heart. The problem was, I felt alone. I would think to myself, "I have it all, but I have nothing."

The one thing I truly desired was missing; I wanted to be married. I would ask myself questions like, *What's wrong with me?* and *Does God want me to be alone?* When we do

Self-Image

not have God's perspective on ourselves, we are willing to settle for less than God wants to give us.

Maybe as a single woman, you have asked yourself some of the same questions. At one point I said, "If I can't find Mr. Right, I will settle for Mr. Half-Right." Now you know that is not the will of God concerning you or me. I want to encourage you to continue to seek God. When I began to see myself as God saw me, I realized I was who God made me to be. God said I was not just good, but very good. *"God saw all that he had made, and it was very good"* (Genesis 1:31).

When I go back to read entries in my journals dating back to 1989, I am amazed. I can see when the transformation took place in my life. My self-image changed, and I no longer saw myself as lonely. Even though it would be another two years before I would meet my husband, I did not feel alone. I knew God had a plan and a purpose for my life, and I would rather wait on God than to rush and make a mistake. You must see yourself walking in the plan and purpose of God's will for your life.

Focus on doing God's will and not so much on yourself. You too will experience the transformation I experienced over seventeen years ago. I was a believer who loved God and was faithful to my church responsibilities. I gave my tithes and always a good offering without fail. I taught Sunday school and accomplished outreach and evangelism. I led many to Christ but was living an unfulfilled life.

I needed to know who I was, so I had to go back to the one who created me. If you are searching today, wanting to know your purpose, ask God, your creator.

One day my sister-in-law had a problem with her Honda. Her husband took the car to several mechanics. None of them could find a problem with the car. Sometimes the car would start, and sometimes it wouldn't. All the mechanics would check the car but could not find anything wrong. Then he took the car to the Honda dealership, where the problem was diagnosed and corrected. It was not a major repair, but because the other mechanics were not the makers of the car, they could not identify the problem.

If we want to know about ourselves, we have to go to the source—not our girlfriends or our spouses. Ask God. He created you in His image, and He has the manual. All the details of your life are included. *"So God created man in his own image, in the image of God he created him; male and female he created them"* (Genesis 1:27).

Just as many others were, I was searching for something to make me feel better. I met with the Air Force recruiter and applied to join the flight nurse program. I did not meet the height and weight requirements. Even when we do not realize it, God is looking out for us. I was looking for answers in all the wrong places. I was going to the wrong people to affirm me and make me feel better.

I stress the fact that I was a Christian because many times we think people who know God have it all together. As believers, sometimes we pretend so other people will respect us. We do not want others to know how we really feel. We think, *If they really knew what I was like, they wouldn't like me.* If you want to be delivered, we must first admit that we have a problem.

I loved God but did not really know who I was. I did not know that my ability to reap the promises of God was wrapped up in how I saw myself. I did not realize that deep down I felt that God had forgotten about me and did not understand my needs. I want to remind you today of the truth of God's Word. He has not forgotten you; in fact, He knows your name. *"Do not fear, for I have redeemed you; I have called you by name; you are Mine!"* (Isaiah 43:1 NASB). Women of

Self-Image

Promise, I speak to your destiny. You are a child of God. Listen to who God's Word says you are and how much you mean to Him.

> *Yet to all who received him, to those who believed in his name, he gave the right to become children of God* (John 1:12).

> *For we are God's workmanship, created in Christ Jesus to do good works, which God prepared in advance for us to do* (Ephesians 2:10).

> *You were bought at a price. Therefore honor God with your body* (1 Corinthians 6:20).

> *For you know that it was not with perishable things such as silver or gold that you were redeemed from the empty way of life handed down to you from your forefathers, but with the precious blood of Christ, a lamb without blemish or defect* (I Peter 1:18-19).

You were not redeemed with silver or gold; you were purchased by the precious blood of Christ. He paid the price for us when He hung on the cross. You are worth so much to God; do not sell yourself short.

If you are trusting God for a mate, do not settle for less. Let God give you the one He has chosen for you. I would go out regularly with the nice young men I would meet, but I was determined not to step out of God's will concerning my destiny. When you understand your value, you will want to wait for God's best.

I made a list of seven qualities I was believing God for in my husband. I prayed over my list daily, and I was not about to settle for less than God had promised me. I knew I was worth God's best because my heart was to please Him. *"For the Lord God is a sun and shield; the Lord bestows favor and honor; no good thing does he withhold from those whose walk is blameless"* (Psalm 84:11).

God knows our hearts. When your heart is to please Him, He will honor that. I am convinced the hand of God guided me even when I wanted to go my own way. I committed my heart to God, and I prayed diligently for His protection. He honored my prayer and granted my request. Even when I desired to go in the wrong direction, I had already prayed, "Lord keep me in the center of your will." As I prayed over my list of qualifications for a mate, I believed God would grant my request. And yes, ladies, I was prepared to wait. I told God, "Lord if I never get married, I will still love You and serve You."

Can God trust you? Do you love Him enough to wait for His promises? When He gives you the man of your dreams, will you still put God first? Will you continue to seek His face for direction?

The Scripture tells us that God has given us the power to call things that are not as though they were,

> *As it is written: I have made you a father of many nations. He is our father in the sight of God, in whom he believed—the God who gives life to the dead and calls things that are not as though they were* (Romans 4:17).

You can change the way you see yourself.

Speak the words out loud so you can hear them. Call yourself what God calls you. God calls you "friend." See your dreams and speak them. Declare your dream to God. As you talk to yourself, you will develop a new image on the inside. Say what God said about you. God says you are the head and not the tail; you are always on the top and not the bottom. *"The Lord will make you the head, not the tail. If you pay at-*

Self-Image

tention to the commands of the Lord your God that I give you this day and carefully follow them, you will always be at the top, never at the bottom" (Deuteronomy 28:13).

I am the righteousness of God in Christ Jesus. *"God made him who had no sin to be sin for us, so that in him we might become the righteousness of God"* (2 Corinthians 5:21). You have to see yourself as God sees you. In Scripture we read about the infirmed woman in Luke 13:10-13. Jesus spoke to what she could and would become. He spoke to her destiny.

> *On a Sabbath Jesus was teaching in one of the synagogues, and a woman was there who had been crippled by a spirit for eighteen years. She was bent over and could not straighten up at all. When Jesus saw her, he called her forward and said to her, "Woman, you are set free from your infirmity." Then he put his hands on her, and immediately she straightened up and praised God.*

When you feel unwanted, know that you are wanted and loved. Jesus called the infirmed woman forth, and He proclaimed her freedom. Notice that she had to come when Jesus called her. He waited for her, and He is waiting for you today. You are special to Him. He loves you. You are valuable. He is calling out to you. Will you come to Him? God has already put on record how He feels about you. *"And the Lord has declared this day that you are his people, his treasured possession as he promised, and that you are to keep all his commands"* (Deuteronomy 26:18). God wants to give us His view of life. He wants to enable us to love ourselves as He does, so that we can love others the same way.

The enemy tries to take advantage of the vulnerability of women. When we read the creation story in the book of Genesis, we see Eve's vulnerability. The serpent took advantage of her exposed state. This is why it is so important that we know who we are. Let's look at the dialogue between Eve and the serpent in Genesis 3:1-6.

The serpent appeared out of nowhere to Eve in the garden. The serpent was crafty and sneaky. Eve was innocent and naïve. When the serpent spoke to Eve regarding what God had said, she did not seem surprised.

Eve responded by repeating the positive words that God had said. Eve knew the tree in the middle of the garden was off-limits to her and Adam. In fact, God had told them not to touch that tree. This is when satan lied to her: "You will not surely die!" The serpent boldly denied the truth of what God had said. It appears to me that satan was calling God a liar.

What satan did in the garden he is still doing today. He argued with Eve regarding God's motives. How many times does the enemy try to make you believe that you deserve better, that you are not getting all of what belongs to you, and there must be more to life.

The issue facing Eve is the same one facing you today—that is an issue of obedience to the Word of God. The enemy will offer you temptations, many of which will not hurt you. But if you are acting in disobedience, I guarantee you that you will be hurt in the end.

If Eve had understood her purpose, and if she could have seen herself as God saw her, she would have had no need to listen to satan. When we think we are not good enough, and when we think we deserve more, satan uses our weakness to attempt to overcome us. In other words, if satan can get us to see lack in the way God created us, then he can appeal to our sense of desire.

If we see ourselves as defected in any way, then we are open to the lies of the enemy. That is why it is imperative that we commit to memory the Word of God. When the enemy

Self-Image

talks to us, we have the Word of God to give back to him. David speaks of hiding the Word of God in your heart in Psalms 119:11.

If Eve had really known her worth, she would have known that she was already wise. She would have known that she was everything God had created her to be. Nothing was missing and nothing was broken.

God created us for a purpose; we are impregnated with destiny. We have to give birth to our purpose. As painful as giving birth may be, we must focus more on the outcome and focus less on the process. Begin to thank God for who you are and start appreciating yourself. The true beauty of a woman is her spirit.

Friends, you need to know your own self-worth. God has adorned you inwardly, which is where your real beauty lies. The true beauty of a woman is the part of her you cannot see with the physical eye.

Marriage is not a guarantee that you will experience fulfillment in your life. As a married woman, you may be in a covenant relationship, while your spouse is not covering you. When your husband fails to pray for you regularly, you are left uncovered.

Your husband may be making frequent withdrawals from you emotionally, without making any deposits toward filling the empty places of your heart. You may be in a marriage that is draining you, and you feel desperate and alone.

God has called husbands to be the head of their homes and to speak into the lives of their wives. *"For the husband is the head of the wife as Christ is the head of the church, his body, of which he is the Savior"* (Ephesians 5:23).

A husband is to encourage his wife and to affirm her in all

she does. He is to love her and help her accomplish everything God intended for her to accomplish. He is to motivate her to be all that she can be. When all is said and done, the wife is a reflection of her husband. If she is weary and broken, than we must examine her relationship with her husband.

> *Husbands, in the same way be considerate as you live with your wives, and treat them with respect as the weaker partner and as heirs with you of the gracious gift of life, so that nothing will hinder your prayers* (1 Peter 3:7).

If you are married, your husband holds the key for the blessing of your family. His obedience can cause the promises of God to flow freely in your family; and his disobedience can hinder the promises of God for your family. He can change the course of your marriage by moving into proper position. A husband needs to love his wife, even when she is not so lovely. He needs to speak positively to her.

Wives, strive to do what God has called you to do in relation to your mate. You have a responsibility to help your husband. Help him fulfill dreams; after all, God did create you as a helper. *"The Lord God said, 'It is not good for the man to be alone, I will make a helper suitable for him'"* (Genesis 2:18). When we fail to fulfill our individual responsibilities in our marriage, we open the door for sin to enter our marriages.

When these kinds of affirmations are not received within the boundaries of marriage, often one or both people will find them outside of the marriage. There is a need in all of us to know who we really are. If you are not receiving the positive stroking you need in your marriage, let me encourage you to seek God. He is a friend that sticks closer than a brother. *"A man of many companions may come to ruin, but there is a friend who sticks closer than a brother"* (Proverbs 18:24).

God will fill any place that is lacking in your life. You may

Self-Image

feel like you have a hole in your heart, but the hole is not so big that the love of God cannot fill it. If your mate is not telling you how special you are, allow God to speak His Word to you. You are special to Him, and He loves you always. He will affirm to you who you really are.

You were chosen by God before the creation of the world. Before the foundation of the world, God had you in mind. He placed you in the world according to His purpose at His appointed time. He waited until the time was right to bring you forth. If your self-image is distorted, your whole perception of life is distorted. Do not allow what anyone says or does not say to cause you to doubt who you are in God. If you doubt who you are in God, you will never fulfill the call of God on your life. You will fail to be all that God has called you to be and fail to do all that He has called you to do.

When God created woman, He caused a deep sleep to fall upon Adam

> *So the Lord God caused the man to fall into a deep sleep and while he was sleeping, he took one of the man's ribs and closed up the place with flesh. Then the Lord God made a woman from the rib he had taken out of the man, and he brought her to the man* (Genesis 2:21-22).

God did not need Adam's help; He put Adam to sleep. Adam had seen all the beautiful animals God had created. He saw the waters and the skies and the wonder of it all. But, Adam had not seen anything like what God was doing now.

He brought the woman He made to Adam. She was created for a purpose. Remember, God made Adam from the dust; but when God prepared to make woman, He did not go back to the dirt. We are a special edition created by the hands of a loving God. We are women of influence and power. We have the ability to change our circumstances and our situations.

Never look to others to make you feel good about yourself and do not allow anyone to make you feel bad about yourself. You are complete in Christ, and in Him you have been made complete. Nothing is missing. Learn to be content with what you have, and be content with who you are in Christ.

> *I know what it is to be in need, and I know what it is to have plenty. I have learned the secret of being content in any and every situation, whether well fed or hungry, whether living in plenty or in want* (Philippians 4:12).

You have a rich inheritance. God has created you uniquely as a woman. If you do not know who you are in Christ, it will hold you back from what God has called you to do. For example, I felt inadequate to minister to the many women God would put in my life. I came from a very sheltered background; I grew up in a strict Christian home, and my life experiences were limited. I felt I had nothing to offer women who dealt with addictions, abuse, and those who had suffered other mishaps in their lives. As I began to seek God and allow Him to use me to minister to these women, the most amazing things began to happen.

Women who had held onto anger and bitterness for years were being delivered. Women who struggled with issues I had never experienced were delivered. When we allow God to take control and use us, there is no inadequacy in Him. Many times we are made to feel that we cannot help a person unless we have lived their story. I do not agree with that. While a testimony of deliverance is great, so is a testimony that God kept me from addictions.

I marvel even today at the goodness of God when women tell me how they have been blessed by my teaching. When we

Self-Image

stop looking at our natural abilities and start to focus on our spiritual abilities, we can make a difference in the lives of others. When God calls you to do something, it is something that you will need His help to accomplish. When we can point people to Jesus by showing them His love, He will do the rest. Somebody said, "People don't care how much you know until they know how much you care."

If you are having a problem with self-image/self-worth, you need to surround yourself with four kinds of people: You should have an intercessor, a person who will take your needs and hold them up to the Lord. You need a mentor, a person who can affirm you. You should also have a truth teller; everyone needs one person in their life who will tell them the truth. Last but not least, you need a pastor, one who will make sense out of life and give you God's perspective. These four people will pour into you and cause you to see yourself as God sees you. *"And have put on the new self, which is being renewed in knowledge in the image of its Creator"* (Colossians 3:10).

If you are searching for your true self, search no longer. In the Word of God you will find your true identity. You are not an alien to God, and your feelings are not unfamiliar to Him. He created you in His own image. Every desire that you have the Creator can fill. Remember, He is enough.

Prayer

Dear Heavenly Father, help me to see myself as You see me. I know You can fill every area of my life that is lacking with Your love. When I start to speak negatively of myself, please remind me that I was created in Your image. I pray today that You would remove all the blinders from my eyes that I might see myself as You see me. Remove negative thoughts from my mind so that I might think about myself as

Seven Blessing Blockers

You think of me. I pray for positive people to surround me today, people who love You. I pray for people in my life who will speak Your truth in my ears. I pray for a mentor who will affirm me. I pray for an intercessor who will keep me lifted in prayer. I also pray for a pastor of Your choosing for me who can help me make sense of this world and how it relates to my life. I declare the truth of Your Word over my life. According to Psalm 139:14, I am fearfully and wonderfully made. I thank You for transforming my way of thinking. In Jesus' name I pray. Amen.

Chapter 9

Holding Onto the Past

Five years ago, we moved to the Tampa Bay area from Maryland. Coming to terms with the move was not easy for me. I was in Tampa in body, but every other part of me was still in Maryland. I could not understand why God would move us just after we had built our dream home. I thought, *Why now, just as my real estate career is beginning to soar?* After being on a waiting list for two years, our girls were finally starting the private school for which we had waited. My husband's salary was at its highest and climbing. *God, what are you doing with us?* In my prayer time, I would ask God, *Why? Why now?* It was not that I was unhappy about moving, I just wanted to understand why at this time in our lives God would allow this to happen.

Ebony, my nine-year-old (at the time) daughter said to me, "Mom, you will never step into your future until you let go of the past." Out of the mouth of my baby came truth.

At that time Jesus said, I praise you, Father, Lord of heaven and earth, because you have hidden these things from the wise and the learned , and revealed them to little children (Matthew 11:25).

It was at that moment that I made a decision. The question was, did I want to walk into my destiny or remain in the past? It was clear to me I had to allow God to do what He does best.

My prayer changed. No more, "Why did we have to leave Maryland?" Instead, I asked, "What do you want me to do in Tampa?" It would be nearly two years later that God would begin to reveal to me on a daily basis that He always had my best interests at heart. Friends, as long as you hold onto the past, you will prevent God's promises from being fulfilled in your life. *"For I know the plans I have for you, declares the Lord, plans to prosper you and not to harm you, plans to give you hope and a future"* (Jeremiah 29:11). The Lord did know. Now when I look back, I can see many of the blessings that could have been delayed by my disobedience.

Friends, God knows what He is doing. You can trust Him. His plan is good; it is not to harm you, but to give you hope. Even in the midst of your struggle, focus on the plan that God has for you. It might not look like you are being victorious, but if God has made you a promise, you have to know that He will carry you through this time.

The good news for me is that this is just the beginning, and I am on schedule for great and wonderful blessings. *"However, as it is written: No eye has seen, no ear has heard, no mind has conceived what God has prepared for those who love him"* (1 Corinthians 2:9).

There are some doors that need to be closed so that God can open new doors in our lives. Do not allow your past to hold you back from what God has called you to do or where He has called you to be. We learn from our past.

We treasure the good and forget the bad. Do not ever rest and be satisfied with past accomplishments. There is always another level to which God wants to take you. We can learn

Holding Onto the Past

from our past experiences. It is my past experiences that have made me the person I am today. Some of them were challenging experiences, but I am pretty happy with the person I am today, so I would not change a thing.

Many times God will call us away from conditions that may have been pleasant to us. Circumstances can be going well for us, and God will say, "Release them." I can tell you times in my life when I have had to let go of things I believe God had given me. But I can also tell you that when I was obedient, God gave them back to me. The difference was, there were no strings attached.

Sometimes we hold on so tightly to things. God may want to put something different in your hand, but your hands are closed. When you open your hand to receive the new, you are releasing the old. The interesting thing about a closed hand is that nothing can be put into it, and it is equally as difficult to remove anything from it.

Anything you give up for the cause of Christ you can be assured that God will give it back to you, or He has something better for you. The Scripture teaches us that if we lose our life for Christ, we will gain it again (Matthew 10:39).

It has been the trying of my faith that has increased my faith. Because of the trials God has brought me through, I trust Him more each day. Any time God has called you to do something, there is a process through which you must walk.

We are filled with so many talents and gifts to which we have yet to give birth. Like any good thing that God desires to bring forth in us, the enemy desires to destroy it. This is not the time to look back; our days are short, and Jesus is soon to come. Our lives are so stressed and filled with things to do. I have never before encountered so many people who just want to give up. Many of them are saying, "I can't take it anymore."

God's Word assures us we can always come to Him in our time of need and despair. When challenges come in your life, and they will, sometimes you will feel like turning around. Remember, God has created you with purpose, and even in the hard times, He is there. Stay focused, do not look back, and keep your eye on the prize.

Do you not know that in a race all the runners run, but only one gets the prize? Run in such a way as to get the prize (1 Corinthians 9:24).

Nothing is wasted with God. For every event that He allows, there is a purpose. God does not do anything without purpose. Even when I do not understand and have tears streaming down my face, I will trust God because I know He has a plan. As a result of trusting Him, the freedom that I now experience in Christ has freed me from regrets.

God wants to use you just as you are. Stressed, angry, or depressed—whatever you are feeling—God can take those feelings and make you a great witness for Him. There is something from God inside of you. In the midst of your confusion, God desires you to give birth to His plan and promise for your life. Now is the time to push forward, forgetting that which is behind. Press forward; God desires to make you a new creature. *"Therefore, if anyone is in Christ, he is a new creation; the old has gone, the new has come!"* (2 Corinthians 5:17). He does not want you holding onto the past, but He does want you reaching for the future.

When we allow others to depend on us, we are holding them back. Letting people become too dependent on you is not helpful to them. You only hinder them from growing and developing an intimate relationship with Jesus Christ. In the long run, they grow to resent you because you never allowed them to develop. I know it is difficult to understand, and at times it may not seem like it, but God really does have great plans for you. We have to learn to live each day trusting God and enjoying every moment.

We lived in Northern California for a year because my husband's company sent him there. I constantly wanted to go back to the East Coast. It was no fun being that far from home, pregnant, and with a toddler. After giving birth to our second daughter in California, I had a newborn and a toddler to take care of.

Most of my days were filled with regrets and desires to go back home. Thanks to my husband and his explorer's attitude, we did manage to see many interesting places while we were living in Santa Clara, California. I must admit it was pretty nice to be on Santa Cruz beach on New Year's Day while our family and friends in the Washington, D.C. area were experiencing an ice storm that shut down the federal government for a few days.

When we moved back to the East Coast, I realized how much more enjoyable my West Coast experience could have been if I would have just allowed myself to enjoy it. Life is too short; do not spend your time looking back and holding onto the past. Live each day to the fullness and appreciate every moment. My family certainly understood that all too well when my mother-in-law suddenly passed away while we were in California.

Friend, I want you to enjoy life to the fullest. Do not make the mistakes I made. I struggled for years with issues in my life that did not need to be a problem but nevertheless were a hindrance to me.

Yes, I believed God, but I was so caught up in yesterday. Once I understood that today was all I had, then I was able to stop dwelling on what I felt like yesterday or what happened or did not happen yesterday. I spent a lot of days letting other people decide how I was going to feel, and I let the actions of others control me.

When I began to trust God for tomorrow, my life took a miraculous turn. Now when I read some of my journal entries from years back, I have to ask God to forgive me for not letting go sooner. One of the reasons I held on to the past for so long was my lack of faith.

I lacked the ability to trust God with every part of my life. Yes, I was a believer, a teacher of God's Word, yet I lacked faith. It was through my life's experiences that I learned to trust God completely. Yes, some of those experiences I despised, but I now see that they were necessary for me to learn the lessons well. When you learn a lesson, you do not have to repeat the class.

Thank God, I have learned and finally understand. God is in control. He knows everything, including the future. I can let go and let God take the reins of my life. You can too. Do not spend as many years as I did searching for answers. Trust God; He has the answers, and it does not matter what the question is.

I spend much of my time helping and speaking into the lives of young women who are searching for purpose in their lives. I see myself in most of them because I have been there. I attended a conference last year where I heard Joyce Meyer preach a sermon entitled "Don't Go There." I have been there, and I do not plan to go back. I do not want you to go there, and if you are there, I want to help you come back from there. There is a place of misery where your mind is confused. There is a place where you do not know which end is up. You spend most of your time struggling to let go, but you do not know how. Where is the place you call "there"? For me it was a place of fear and anxiety. It was a place of little faith and much despair.

Holding Onto the Past

Once I understood God's promises for my life, I made a decision to walk in obedience. I knew if I was obedient and followed His Word, I would be blessed. The blessing is not geographical. I am blessed.

I now understand that it did not matter if I were in Maryland, California, or Tampa, Florida—I would be blessed. I do not have to be overly concerned if moving would negatively impact my children because the Bible says, *"the fruit of my womb would be blessed"* (Deuteronomy 28:4). Simply because my children were connected to me, they would be blessed.

If you want to be blessed, get connected with someone who is living her purpose. Do what you see her do. Talk like she talks, and praise like she praises. Follow someone who knows where she is going. Let positive words come out of your mouth; hold your head high when you walk.

You might have had a rocky start, but you do not have to stay there. God wants to move you from where you are. He wants to take you to a higher level. He wants to make you the head and not the tail. It does not matter where you start in life, what does matter is where you end up. Trust and believe God's Word. God does not want you to go through life feeling anxious. Anxiety can cause you to abort your destiny.

Let God bring you out of the storm. Every winding and crooked road you go down has a purpose. God uses the experiences of our lives—good and bad—to steer us toward our purpose. When you dwell too much in the past, it can cause you to become angry with God. Learn from the past and move on into your future. You cannot successfully focus on the future until you have learned from the past.

The enemy would have you believe that the reason certain things have happened to you is because God is angry with you. The Word tells us that God's thoughts toward you are thoughts of peace. They are not thoughts of anger. God does not want to harm you, but He does want to prosper you.

God wants you to succeed and thrive. He wants you to grow in a vigorous way. God is more interested in changing you than in changing your circumstances. You can ask, "Why *me*? Why *this*? Why *now*?" Or, you can learn from your experiences. You are not responsible for what happens *to* you, but you are responsible for what happens *in* you.

When God tells you something, do not look at your circumstances. Our circumstances can look dim, but when we look to God, we can see the light at the end of the tunnel. Hold fast to whatever God's Word has proclaimed to be the truth. Do not receive from any other source; let God's Word be the final word. God's Word declares that you are blessed, so guess what? You are blessed.

> *I make known the end from the beginning, form ancient times what is still to come. I say, my purpose will stand and I will do all that I please. From the east I summon a bird of prey, from a far off land a man to fulfill my purpose. What I have said that will I bring about. What I have planned that will I do"* (Isaiah 46:10-11).

God is faithful to perform His Word. So the next time satan tells you God has forgotten you, tell the devil, "I am who God says I am, and I can do what God says I can do." When the enemy tries to get me off focus, I remind him and myself that God has a plan for my life. I now understand that when the enemy comes after me, he is coming after the Word that has been deposited in me, that Word that tells me God is for me and I am blessed.

The devil comes to destroy the promises that have been spoken over your life. He knows if he can kill the promise, then the dream that is on the inside of you will die. However,

Holding Onto the Past

the Scripture is very clear, and we can always stand on God's Word. *"No weapon forged against you will prevail"* (Isaiah 54:17). Tell the enemy, "Come on, devil. Give it your best shot; God's Word says you will not prevail." If I remain in obedience to what God has called me to do, I cannot fail. I must purpose in my heart to obey God always. Now is the time to let go whatever you might be holding onto from your past.

Many times we hold onto unhealthy relationships from the past, causing us to become emotionally handicapped. We cannot allow our past to become a crutch for us. When we lean on others, we are not leaning on God.

God is the one who heals you and sets you free. Your friends can support you, but God is the only one who can keep you from falling. God takes your blame, your mistakes, and your faults all away. You do not have to blame yourself for circumstances that arise. You need to give all of your blame and your shame away to God because He wants it!

Sometimes after the loss of a love one, it is difficult to let go of the past. Often we remain in the grief longer than we should. We linger too long, focusing on what was lost. I lost someone very close to me in a tragic accident very suddenly. It was very difficult, and I wondered if I would ever come to terms with her death. In the end, I had the realization that God was in control of my past, present, and future. I had to understand that she had fulfilled her purpose here on earth and had returned to her heavenly Father just as I would do one day.

Grief can be unhealthy if we allow it to consume us. I do not know why bad things happen to good people. There will always be something that cannot be explained, but we must make the choice to continue. Grief is a complicated, multi-dimensional, individual process that can never be generalized in steps.

Seven Blessing Blockers

If you ever have the opportunity to minister to a person who has lost a loved one, the best thing you can do is listen and support them. Pray not only *for* them, but also pray *with* them. Assure them that God has not forgotten them and He does care. Sometimes we just have to make the decision to go on without knowing why. There are some things we have to just accept and file away as part of our past. I am not asking you to forget loved ones you have lost. You have the memories always, but you must give yourself permission to be released from the past so you can move on to reap the promises of your future.

In our lives, we have many unfortunate events that take place, but God has promised to set us free from every curse of the past. God has promised that He would never leave us. He wants to restore and give us a complete healing. It is in the brokenness of our lives that God does some of His best work. He desires to restore us to a whole person—well in body, emotions, and spirit.

Our past is behind us, and we must look to the future. I am convinced that my best days are in front of me. Tomorrow is a new day with new opportunities, new dreams, and new roads to travel. Do not let your past hold you back. You will not be able to take the old stuff into the new place God is taking you.

If God has given you a vision to move ahead, do not get comfortable in the past. We have to press past all the hurts and disappointments of our past and move into our future. God wants to put something new in our hands, but we must open our hands and release what we are holding onto. When we open our hands and release the old, God can place something new in its place.

Wounds of the past will often leave a scar. These scars are left from the past only as a reminder of the goodness of God.

As long as you continue to lick the wound, the wounds will not heal, and a scar cannot form. It is important that a scar forms over a wound. That is why you must release everything to God and not continue to linger in past misery. The scar forms as a reminder to you of where God has brought you from and what He has brought you through. You cannot change the past, but in the present, you can give God everything.

Prayer

Dear Heavenly Father, I pray for a release from everything in my past that seeks to hold me back. I desire to move into my destiny and to receive every promise You have for me in Your Word. I pray today that anything that in my life that does not honor You will be revealed to me. After it has been revealed, I pray for the strength to let it go. When I think I have let it go, I find myself continuing to focus on _____.

But, I pray that this will be the last day I focus on _____. I know I cannot move into my future while holding onto the past. I trust You, God, and I know that everything that has happened to me was meant to bring me to this place in You. I now receive the past as a lesson learned, and I release myself to move into my destiny. When I think of the past, let me think of it as lessons that I have learned and not as mistakes that I have made. My deepest desire is to fulfill Your call on my life. Keep me listening to hear Your voice, and keep me humble enough to follow it. I have no more questions of "why?" I declare today that You are enough for me. In Jesus' name I pray. Amen.

Chapter 10

Test of Obedience

I tremble when I think of the times I tried to walk outside of God's will for my life. It was and continues to be God's mercy that keeps me. I often think of God's mercy and protection that I experienced during my dating years. A few of the young men I would meet, I would think to myself, "I could settle for this one." But God in His divine providence would somehow move that one out of my life. Sometimes it would be as simple as losing a telephone number or a scheduling conflict.

At times, I wanted to run from God by moving geographically, but He showed up no matter where I went. It does not matter where we go; we cannot flee from the presence of the Lord. God is everywhere and in every place at the same time. We cannot hide from God. He sees everything that we do.

Many times it is easier to disobey than to obey. It is easy to say no when God wants us to say yes. When we say no, there are no conditions attached—or so we think. It is our obedience that gains us favor with God.

Even when my flesh wanted to be disobedient, my heart's

Test of Obedience

desire was to obey. I believe it is because of an obedient heart that I was spared and protected. When I look back, I thank God that He knew my heart.

When you commit your life to God and ask Him to take full control, you can trust Him. God will hold you up even when you should be falling down. He is always there to direct you. *"Never will I leave you, never will I forsake you"* (Hebrews 13:5).

The ultimate test of obedience is found in Genesis 22:2-18. God told Abraham to take his only son Isaac to Moriah, meaning where the Lord provides or where the Lord appears. Abraham had one son by Hagar, but only Isaac was born as "only begotten." Remember, Isaac was the son God had promised Abraham. So in essence, God was telling Abraham to sacrifice His promise.

Have you ever wanted something so badly that you would do anything to get it, and then when you got it, you had to relinquish it? I can image what Abraham must have felt. "God gave me a son, now He wants me to sacrifice him."

God will ask us to give up what we love most to see if we will obey. Abraham was obedient. He saddled his donkey and took with him two servants and his son Isaac. Abraham told his servants, "Stay here with the donkey while my son and I go over there." The interesting thing is that Abraham told the servant, "We will return."

Now I ask myself, how did Abraham know he and Isaac would return? Some Bible historians say that Abraham was lying to the servant. One scholar said that he was delusional. I believe Abraham remembered what God had said. God told Abraham that He would create a nation through Isaac.

Abraham believed what God had said. He believed that even if he killed his son, God would bring him back to life.

Friends, when God says something, we can take it to the bank. We do not have to second-guess God. His Word is settled, and He does not change.

When Abraham and his son got to the place, Isaac said, "Where is the lamb for the sacrifice?" But Abraham, a man of faith, replied, "God will provide." You may be in the valley of decision at this moment, but I want you to know, God will provide.

When we are committed to being obedient and following the plan of God for our lives, we do not have to worry. God will provide. We must trust Him and be willing to obey whatever He asks us to do.

As Abraham prepared to sacrifice the son God promised him, God spoke from heaven and said, "Do not lay your hand." The Scripture records that Abraham was just about to strike his son, and God stopped his hand.

Certainly, God knew how this would all turn out long before that moment. Friends, God knows how things are going to turn out in your life. He his standing with you watching and showing His appreciation for your obedience as you walk through this life.

God will ask us to do things that we will never need to do. He just wants to know if we are willing to be obedient. Many times a yes to God will stop the turmoil in our lives. Life becomes difficult when we fight against what God has asked us to do.

When God told Abraham to take his only son and offer him as a sacrifice, Abraham believed and trusted God. He knew what God had promised him. He also knew that if God had made a promise, God would keep it. Abraham kept his eye on the promise. It does not matter what the situation looks like, we have to remember to obey the Word of God. Because of Abraham's obedience, God showed up.

Test of Obedience

When we look at obedience and disobedience, it is not only nonbelievers that disobey. Believers are sometimes just as guilty as nonbelievers of practicing disobedience. If we want to reap the promises of God's Word, we must obey. Always choose to obey God; nothing ever gets better when you make a choice to disobey.

Disobedient Christians will not reap all the promises of God for their lives, but when we are obedient, we can expect to take over the land.

Do what is right and good in the Lord's sight, so that it may go well with you and you may go in and take over the good land that the Lord promised on oath to your forefathers (Deuteronomy 6:18).

God has promised us grace for every trial we face, but a disobedient Christian is not likely to experience the grace that has been provided for her.

No temptation has seized you except what is common to man. And God is faithful; he will not let you be tempted beyond what you can bear. But when you are tempted, he will also provide a way out so that you can stand up under it (1 Corinthians 10:13).

And God is able to make all grace abound to you, so that in all things at all times, having all that you need, you will abound in every good work (2 Corinthians 9:8).

God has promised to supply our every need, but the believer who will not obey God is likely to suffer want. *"And my God will meet all your needs according to his glorious riches in Christ Jesus"* (Philippians 4:19).

An obedient Christian is an overcoming Christian. *"No, in all these things we are more than conquerors through him who loved us"* (Romans 8:37). A disobedient child of God can expect to live in defeat all the days of her disobedient life.

When we desire the blessing's Giver more than the blessing, we are in the proper position. As pastors, my husband and I have been called by God to serve. We must be obedient, but it is not always easy. There are times when my servitude is with joy and other times when it's a chore for me. (I'm keeping it real.)

Sometimes I struggle with whether or not my service is willful service. The call of God to serve is one that I must commit to daily. I recognize that it is not my place to make judgments about who is worthy of service. Even when I am discouraged because I have tried to help someone who continues down a destructive path, I must remain focused. God will hold me accountable for my obedience to Him.

Someone asked me, "If God called you, will you not like what you are doing?" Our flesh is always in opposition to the spirit. Just because God called me does not mean my flesh will want to comply.

The highest level of commitment to spiritual growth is an act of obedience to God's Word. In the beginning, God gave Adam and Eve a command to be fruitful and multiply. We too have a task to replenish the earth with people who believe in God.

Evangelism began in the heart of God at creation. Growth is essential for life; if we do not grow, we will die. Jesus came to seek and save the lost. He came to be a light in darkness and to bring life to all. Jesus instructed the leaders He chose to go and make believers of everyone. The great commission of every born-again believer is to duplicate until Jesus returns.

Therefore go and make disciples of all nations, baptizing them in the name of the Father and of the Son and of the Holy Spirit, and teaching them to obey everything I commanded you. And surely I am with you always, to the very end of the age (Matthew 28:19-20).

We are expected not only to know the Great Commission, but also to be obedient and truly become people who will spread the Gospel. The fruit of our obedience is the many souls that will be won to the kingdom. My friend, God promised He would not leave you as you walk in obedience to win the lost to Him.

As believers, we understand that when God calls us, He desires for us to gather others for His kingdom. We have to remain faithful to what we believe God has assigned our hands to do. In your obedience to the Father, you will reap a reward. *"Let us not become weary in doing good, for at the proper time we will reap a harvest if we do not give up"* (Galatians 6:9). Here we see another promise of God. Friends, do not give up; hold on. Continue to sow, but sow your seeds in fertile ground. If you do not sow seeds, there will be no crop for you to reap. Everything we sow eventually bears fruit; it is the law of sowing and reaping. If we sow a bad seed, the harvest will be bad. *"As I have observed, those who plow evil and those who sow trouble reap it"* (Job 4:8).

He who sows wickedness reaps trouble, and the rod of his fury will be destroyed (Proverbs 22:8).

Sow for yourselves righteousness; reap the fruit of unfailing love (Hosea 10:12).

Peacemakers who sow in peace raise a harvest of righteousness (James 3:18).

Obedience is the key to walking in the plan and purpose of God for your life. When God reveals to you His purpose, He usually does it one step at a time; He will not show you all of it at once. Think about it. If God showed you everything, you would say, "No way!" (I know I would.) But as you go through your everyday life, God will show you a glimpse of His plan for you. He will show you just enough to get you excited and entice you to want to know more.

Often when God speaks to me, He only speaks one word. I know from experience that one word from God can be life-changing. The power of one revelation of God, one truth of God released into your spirit, is worth more than studying all day in the flesh. Many times in my life, just one word deposited into my spirit would propel me to soar.

When you are walking in obedience and you do not see the promise being fulfilled, do not panic. Begin to give God praise and thanksgiving as if you have already received the promise.

Remember, as a believer you see things through eyes of faith. Some things have not materialized yet, but we still have faith that it will come to pass. I see the promise through the eyes of the Spirit. God's Word will not return unto Him void. *"So is my word that goes out from my mouth: It will not return to me empty, but will accomplish what I desire and achieve the purpose for which I sent it"* (Isaiah 55:11). When God gives a Word, it is for a purpose.

God desires to fill us with His Word and to do a major, life-changing work in us. If you want to see the promises come to pass in your life, agree with God's Word. Learn to trust His Word above anything or anyone else. God's Word will never fail.

Can we be obedient when God is asking us to do something that is not comfortable? Sometimes the result of obedience is not an improvement in our circumstances, but a strengthening of our faith and a refining of our character. Can

Test of Obedience

we move out of our comfort zones and trust our Lord and Savior Jesus Christ?

To get to your next spiritual level, it will take a new level of faith *"Now faith is being sure of what we hope for and certain of what we do not see"* (Hebrews 11:1). Even when we do not see the promise, we have to trust God. *"We live by faith, not by sight"* (2 Corinthians 5:7).

I remember when we were starting the ministry in Tampa. My husband and I were founders of a ministry in Maryland, and I knew how difficult it was to start a ministry without the necessary funding. I was not looking forward to going down that road again. We initially started having services in our living room with two other families.

There was no room for growth in our home. The Wednesday night Bible Study was extending beyond the living room, and it started to get crowded. When we started looking for a facility to lease, everything was very expensive. My husband felt God was speaking to him to make an offer on this one place we found. I was a bit apprehensive, to say the least.

During our Wednesday night Bible study, he asked the people to plant seeds for the building. There were about five adults present that night in addition to the two of us. Since the attendance was so low that particular night, I thought, *Maybe this is a sign that we are not ready to move.* With that small group, our home would work just fine. That night with five adults present, nearly $10,000 of seed money was sowed for the building—not pledges, but funds that were available the next day.

We indeed walk by faith and not by sight. Walking by sight would have us still meeting in our home, but walking by faith has us in a building. We now have several mid-week services, weekend events, and Sunday evening services. It would not have been feasible for us to hold that many events in our home. Thank God for the faith and vision He gave Pastor Scott, because Pastor Evelyn was a little shaky.

If you struggle with remaining obedient to God, you might need someone to help you become accountable. Get an accountability partner, someone who can encourage you to hang in there. That is what my husband did for me that night at our dining room table with five other adults. He assured me that if God said it, it would come to pass. Sometimes you need someone to help you believe God. The enemy would have you focus on every negative aspect of life. If your mind can be clouded with negative thoughts, then you begin to doubt.

I encourage people to keep a prayer journal so that they can write out their prayer requests. When the request is answered, write out the answer. Do not forget to document the dates of the requests and the dates of the answers. When you start to feel down and thinking about giving up, pick up the prayer journal. As you begin to read and reflect on what God has done for you in the past, it will encourage your heart to remain focused and obedient to the call of God on your life. It is good to have a history with God.

If you want to be blessed abundantly, the power lies in your own hands. God has given you a tool that will release blessings in your life. That tool is obedience. Use it to break from the bondages that hold you captive. A yes to God will open many doors of blessing for you and your family. The Word of God is very specific and convincing in regards to obedience.

> *We know that we have come to know him if we obey his commands. The man who says, I know him, but does not do what he commands is a liar, and the truth is not in him. But if anyone obeys his word, God's love is truly made complete in him. This is how we know we are in him: Whoever claims to live in him must walk as Jesus did* (1 John 2:3-6).

Test of Obedience

Obedience is the key to living as Jesus did. Are you walking as Jesus did in complete obedience and loyalty to God? That is how others know that we love Christ. When we live a life of obedience to Him, it is a true demonstration of our love for Him.

Here is a good motto concerning our relationship with God: obedience is always the best policy. But Samuel said, *"Does the Lord delight in burnt offerings and sacrifices as much as in obeying the voice of the Lord? To obey is better than sacrifice, and to heed is better than the fat of rams"* (1 Samuel 15:22).

It is simple to choose the easy way out. The enemy will whisper in your ear, "Just this once, it will be all right." Anytime you make a decision to disobey God, you can expect nothing good to come from it. The Bible teaches us what God expects from us. When we know what is right to do, then we need to do the right thing. *"Anyone, then, who knows the good he ought to do and doesn't do it, sins"* (James 4:17). In other words, when you know what you should be doing and you choose to do otherwise, you are disobeying, which is sin.

Obedience is necessary. It is not an option if you want to receive the promises of God. We show our love to our heavenly Father by our acts of obedience. *"And this is love: that we walk in obedience to his commands. As you have heard from the beginning, his command is that you walk in love"* (2 John 1:6).

Just as we ask our children to obey, our heavenly Father has asked us to obey. As parents, you know how hurtful it can be when you have a disobedient child. When you give so much to your children and put up with so much from them and then that same child disobeys, it is like a slap in the face. As parents, we want to give good things to our children. There is no reluctance on God's part to bless children, but God does not release His blessings indiscriminately. He will not pour spiritual riches into the lives of rebellious children. When we obey our Father we are saying, "I love you enough to follow Your commands."

One of God's promises as a result of obedience is His presence. The rebellious believer certainly will not experience the sense and enjoyment of God's presence. *"Never will I leave you; never will I forsake you"* (Hebrews 13: 5). God has given unto us exceeding great and precious promises. *"Through these he has given us his very great and precious promises, so that through them you may participate in the divine nature* and escape the corruption in the world caused by evil desires" (2 Peter 1:4). The disobedient believer is not often the recipient of these promises.

When we obey, we can have power over the enemy.

> *Do what is right and good in the Lord's sight, so that it may go well with you and you may go in and take over the good land that the Lord promised on oath to your forefathers, thrusting out all your enemies before you, as the Lord said* (Deuteronomy 6:18-19).

God promised the children of Israel victory over the enemy, if they were obedient. *"If you listen carefully to what he says and do all that I say, I will be an enemy to your enemies and will oppose those who oppose you"* (Exodus 23:22).

The same blessings apply in the life of an obedient believer today. God does not change; neither does His Word. My journey to obedience continues even today as I write this. It is all about the choices we make. God has given us free will, and we can choose to obey or to disobey. Woman of Promise, I speak to your destined state. You are an overcomer. You are more than a conqueror. *"No, in all these things we are more than conquerors through him who loved us"* (Romans 8:37). You are a woman of great value. *"For wisdom is more pre-*

cious than rubies, and nothing you desire can compare with her" (Proverbs 8:11).

Make a solemn vow today to obey God and start reaping the promises of God. The choice is yours. When you make the decision to walk in obedience, you have just opened the door to your blessings. It will not always be an easy choice to make, but do not let anyone or anything keep you from doing what is right. Only you can block your blessings.

Study Guide Questions

Blessing Blocker #1: Unforgiveness

1. When studying forgiveness, what offers you the greatest challenge and why?

___

2. Read Romans 12:2. How does this Scripture apply to forgiveness? Support your answer with a specific detail from your own life.

___

3. What has been your most difficult experience with forgiveness?

___

4. What are some of the reasons we refuse to forgive those who have offended us?

___

5. What does 1 Peter 3:9 say about wanting to get even? Have you ever wanted to get even? Describe a specific event from your life when you wanted to get even. How did you handle it, and what decision did you make?

___

6. How can being unwilling to forgive cause you to abort your destiny? Do you agree or disagree with this statement? Explain.

_____
_____
_____

7. In some cases, it takes a long time to forgive. Why?

_____
_____
_____

8. Are you able to forgive quickly, or does it take a long time? Give a specific example from your life and describe how you handled it.

_____
_____
_____

9. Have you ever had a conversation with God about forgiveness? How did your conversation go? What was the outcome of the conversation?

_____
_____
_____

10. Do you agree or disagree with the following statement? Support your opinion.
"I believe in our lives that when we marry the right person, God has placed that person in our lives to help bring our issues to the surface so the issues can be dealt with appropriately."

_____
_____
_____

11. What is the three-strike rule, and do you have one?
_____
_____
_____

12. How important is forgiveness in getting our prayers answered? Explain.
_____
_____
_____

13. Is forgiveness a one-time act or is it continuous? Explain.
_____
_____
_____

14. What did Peter ask Jesus in Matthew 18:21-22, and what was Jesus' answer?
_____
_____
_____

15. What are some of the adverse affects of harboring unforgiveness in your heart?
_____
_____
_____

16. Why should we be thankful for our enemies? Name some of the ways our enemies help us.
_____
_____
_____

17. Are we able to accomplish true forgiveness of others on our own? Explain your answer.

18. Name one of the blessings of forgiveness. What blessings have you experienced as a result of forgiving someone?

19. Do you have someone that you have not been able to forgive? Say the prayer at the end of the chapter and allow God to do a work in you.

Blessing Blocker #2: Attitude

1. When studying attitude, what offers you the greatest challenge and why?

2. Do a self-evaluation. How would you describe your attitude most of the time?

3. Evaluate Job. What was his attitude?

4. Describe the difference between Ruth's attitude and Naomi's attitude. Which attitude was rewarded by God and how?

5. Ruth teaches single women a very valuable lesson. What is it?

6. What impact can your attitude have on your health? What are some of the physical symptoms of a chronic negative attitude?

7. Because we know God loves us all, how can you obtain God's favor in your life?

8. Give an example of God's favor in your life. Be specific.

9. What does Mark 11:23-24 say to you about your present situation? What is your mountain?

10. Write out a Scripture that speaks to you when you are feeling down.

11. What should you do when negative thoughts come into your mind?

12. Have you ever experienced a contagious attitude? If so, what attitude was it?

13. What have been some of your downfalls as the result of a negative attitude?

14. What have been some of your victories as a result of a positive attitude?

15. Why are so many of our life's events, both negative and positive, directly related to our attitude?

16. Make a prayer list of people you know who have a negative attitude, and include yourself if necessary. Pray the prayer at the end of the chapter for every person on your list.

Blessing Blocker #3: Pride

1. When studying pride, what offers you the greatest challenge and why?

2. How does pride hold us back from the promises of God being manifested in our lives?

3. What is the difference between the pride mentioned in Galatians 6:4 and the pride mentioned in Proverbs 8:13?

4. What are some of the results of allowing pride to dwell in us?

5. Why is it so much easier to see the shortcomings of others than it is to see our own shortcomings?

6. How can your background distort the way you see others?

_____
_____
_____

7. Has your sight been distorted by the way you were raised? Explain.

_____
_____
_____

8. Do you know of anyone who has experienced this form of distorted vision? Explain.

_____
_____
_____

9. How do the Scriptures presented on pride speak to you? Give a specific Scripture reference and how it impacts your thinking.

_____
_____
_____

10. What should our actions be when we recognize a hindrance in someone else's life?

11. When a person owns or desires nice and expensive things, is that considered to be prideful?

_____
_____
_____

12. Why does the author say, "So much of our life is about God"?

_____

13. Do you agree or disagree that trusting God is liberating? Explain.

14. How can we make Galatians 5:22-23 a part of our daily lives?

15. Which fruit of the Spirit do you lack? Explain your answer.

16. Which fruit of the Spirit do you possess in abundance? Explain your answer.

17. What does it mean to be an ambassador of Christ?

18. Does pride affect our worship? If yes, how, and if no, explain your answer.

19. Do you see yourself as a true worshipper?

20. Discuss what this statement means to you. "It is not about the position, it is about the mission."

21. Pray the prayer at the end of the chapter for yourself or someone you know who has a pride issue.

Blessing Blocker #4: Fear

1. When studying fear, what offers you the greatest challenge and why?

2. Why is fear such a strong force in the life of a believer?

3. What is the number one prerequisite to being used by God?

4. When have you allowed fear to hold you back from doing something you really wanted to do? Be specific.
_____
_____
_____

5. Has there ever been a time in your life where you allowed fear to rule? What happened?
_____
_____
_____

6. Has there ever been a time in your life when fear tried to rule, and you were able to conquer the fear? What happened?
_____
_____
_____

7. What is the position of a believer who desires the blessing of God?
_____
_____
_____

8. Matthew 6:33 gives us a fool-proof formula for having our desires met. What is it?
_____
_____
_____

9. Have you ever experienced something that should have caused fear but you were at peace? What was it? How did you react?
_____
_____
_____

10. If you had the opportunity to minister to someone who had a deep-seated fear, how would you help him or her?
_____
_____
_____

11. How can we help people we know who feel alone?
_____
_____
_____

12. In reading 1 Peter 3:1-6, when does the Scripture say we are daughters of Sarah?
_____
_____
_____

13. Do you agree that the underlying cause of most fears is a control issue? If yes, why? And if no, why not?
_____
_____
_____

14. What is a Rhema Word?
_____
_____
_____

15. Have you ever received a Rhema Word from God? If so, when and what was it?
_____
_____
_____

16. What was your response to the Rhema Word that you received?

17. How is fear the opposite of faith?

18. When we are fearful, what are we saying to God? Explain your answer.

19. If we really believe Romans 8:28, then nothing bad ever really happens in the life of a believer. Explain.

20. Read Psalm 139 and think on the awesomeness of God. When in your life have you tried to flee God? What was the result?

21. How and where do we draw the line between fear and caution?

22. When fear says you are not qualified, what is your answer? What should your answer be?

23. What are some of the reasons we live in fear?

24. How can we overcome fear?

25. If you are experiencing fear in any area of your life, pray the prayer at the end of the chapter and allow the Holy Spirit to give you peace.

Blessing Blocker #5: Jealousy

1. When studying jealousy, what offers you the greatest challenge and why?

2. When Joseph's brother tried to destroy him, what were they really trying to destroy? Explain your answer.

3. What was Joseph's perception regarding what his brother did to him? (Read Genesis 47:7.)

4. Do you believe that nothing can happen to you unless God allows it? Explain your answer.

5. Can you recall an event in your life that was meant for evil and God turned it around? Explain.

6. What does 1 Corinthians 13:4 say about love?

7. How are self-worth and jealousy connected?

8. Give an example of jealousy in the Scriptures.

9. Have you ever experienced jealousy? How did you deal with it?

10. If you knew someone was jealous of you, how would you react?
_____
_____
_____

11. How do we teach our children not to be jealous?
_____
_____
_____

12. Why do you believe there is so much jealousy in the world?
_____
_____
_____

13. How does 1 Thessalonians 5:18 speak to a person who is experiencing jealousy?
_____
_____
_____

14. What is the root cause of jealousy?
_____
_____
_____

15. If you or anyone you know is suffering from the green-eyed monster disease, pray the prayer at the end of the chapter.

Blessing Blocker #6: Self-Image

1. When studying self-image, what offers you the greatest challenge and why?

_____
_____
_____

2. What is your real identity?
_____
_____
_____

3. To what is your ability to see yourself as valuable connected?
_____
_____
_____

4. What will improve your self-image?
_____
_____
_____

5. Why do you believe so many women suffer from low self-esteem?
_____
_____
_____

6. If you truly want to know who you are, what do you need to do?
_____
_____
_____

7. What does Isaiah 43:1 say about what God knows about you?
_____
_____
_____

8. How did the enemy take advantage of the vulnerability of Eve?

_____
_____
_____

9. Has the enemy ever taken advantage of your vulnerability? Explain.

_____
_____
_____

10. What should a wife do if her husband is not speaking positive words into her life?

_____
_____
_____

11. How is contentment related to feeling good about who we are?

_____
_____
_____

12. How does not knowing who you are hold you back from receiving the promises of God?

_____
_____
_____

13. How does surrounding yourself with four kinds of people improve your self-image? What four people are mentioned in the book?

_____
_____
_____

14. Do you have these four kinds of people in your life? How have they helped you?

_____
_____
_____

15. Which of the four kinds of people are missing from your life?

_____
_____
_____

16. If you or someone you know suffer from low self-esteem, pray the prayer at the end of the chapter.

Blessing Blocker #7: Holding onto the Past

1. When studying holding onto the past, what offers you the greatest challenge and why?

_____
_____
_____

2. Instead of always asking God "why," what should we be asking Him?

_____
_____
_____

3. What benefit is the past to us?

_____
_____
_____

4. What does Philippians 3:13 say we should do with the past?

_____
_____
_____

5. When ministering to a person who wants to give up, what can you tell him or her?
_____
_____
_____

6. Read Romans 8:28 and fill in the blank in the following sentence.
I know that _____ is working for my good.

7. Have you ever been to a place called there? How did you get out? Do you want to go back?
_____
_____
_____

8. If you want to be blessed, to what kind of people should you be connected?
_____
_____
_____

9. How can leaning on a friend be a hindrance to your growth process?
_____
_____
_____

10. How can letting friends lean on you hinder their growth process?
_____

11. As you consider your presence situation, what are some of the things that can be a hindrance to your growth process?

12. How can you minister to a person who is grieving?

13. Have you ever lost anyone close to you?

14. How did you handle the loss of a loved one? What did you learn?

15. When is grief deemed to be harmful?

16. How can lingering in the past hurt us?

17. Are you lingering in the past? If so, pray the prayer at the end of the chapter.

Daily Devotional Readings

January

1 ....Deuteronomy 29:9
2 ....Proverbs 11:24,25
3 ....Proverbs 10:22
4 ....Malachi 3:10
5 ....Deuteronomy 7:12-14
6 ....Isaiah 32:18,20
7 ....Psalm 115:15
8 ....Numbers 6:24,26
9 ....Deuteronomy 16:15
10 ....Isaiah 49:13
11 ....Ephesians 3:16
12 ....John 14:27
13 ....Psalm 34:19
14 ....Psalm 20:1-2,4
15 ....John 13:1-3
16 ....Philippians 4:13
17 ....2 Thessalonians 1:7
18 ....Isaiah 35:10
19 ....John 6:27
20 ....Philippians 1:20
21 ....John 1:16
22 ....Ephesians 1:3
23 ....Psalm 127:3-5
24 ....Psalm 126:5-6
25 ....Psalm 138:3
26 ....Psalm 5:11
27 ....2 Samuel 22:3
28 ....Psalm 16:5
29 ....Psalm 91:14
30 ....Proverbs 28:1
31 ....Acts 2:38-39

February

1 ....Isaiah 54:13
2 ....Psalm 71:20-21
3 ....Psalm 34:15
4 ....Psalm 128:2
5 ....John 17:15
6 ....Proverbs 2:11
7 ....Acts 2:38-39
8 ....John 15:7
9 ....John 14:13
10 ....Isaiah 30:19
11 ....Hebrews 10:35-36
12 ....Proverbs 12:18
13 .... Psalm 30:2
14 ....Exodus 15:26
15 ....Psalm 107:41
16 ....Hebrews 4:16
17 ....Psalm 32:8
18 ....Deuteronomy 28:12-13
19 ....Proverbs 22:6
20 ....Genesis 12:1-3
21 ....Psalm 27:1
22 ....Mark 10:14,16
23 ....Proverbs 18:10
24 ....Ephesians 1:3
25 ....Psalm 54:4
26 ....Exodus 15:13
27 ....Proverbs 4:11
28 ....Proverbs 15:22
(29)......Isaiah 30:21

March

1 ....Proverbs 17:6
2 ....Psalm 119:105
3 ....Galatians 3:14
4 ....Isaiah 58:11
5 ....Psalms 91:1-2
6 ....Psalm 8:2
7 ....Philippians 4:19
8 ....John 15:7
9 ....Psalm 138:7
10 ....John 14:1
11 ....James 1:5
12 ....Psalm 103:17

13 ....Proverbs 3:1-2
14 ....Psalm 36:7-10
15 ....Jeremiah 29:11-13
16 ....Psalm 103:2-3
17 ....Proverbs 3:21-23
18 ....Deuteronomy 11:18-21
19 ....Psalm 31:3
20 ....Psalm 25:4-5
21 ....Psalm 33:20
22 ....1 Corinthians 2:9-10
23 ....1 John 3:2
24 ....Ephesians 5:1-6
25 ....Psalm 5:11-12
26 ....Psalm 78:4-7
27 ....Genesis 1:27-28
28 ....Exodus 23:25-26
29 ....Ezekiel 34:26
30 ....Isaiah 44:3
31 ....Psalm 23:3

April
1 ....Psalm 43:3
2 ....Psalm 37:25-26
3 ....Deuteronomy 7:6
4 ....Deuteronomy 28:2-8
5 ....Psalm 147:8-11
6 ....Psalm 32:7
7 ....Mark 9:36-37
8 ....2 Corinthians 9:10-11
9 ....Proverbs 3:5-6
10 ....Luke 10:38-42
11 ....Mark 10:29-30
12 ....Proverbs 3:3-4
13 ....Psalm 128:3-4
14 ....Proverb 24:3-4
15 ....Psalm 73:24
16 ....Ephesians 2:22
17 ....3 John 4
18 ....Proverbs 21:20
19 ....Matthew 7:24-25
20 ....John 14:2-3
21 ....Psalm 90:1

22 ....John 16:13
23 ....Psalm 91:9-10
24 ....Psalm 139:14
25 ....Ephesians 2:10
26 ....Proverbs 18:22
27 ....Acts 16:31
28 ....2 Thessalonians 3:3
29 ....John 16:33
30 ....1 Peter 2:4-5

May
1 .... Isaiah 66:13
2 ....Psalm 55:22
3 ....Zephaniah 3:17
4 ....2 Corinthians 5:21
5 ....Jeremiah 24:7
6 ....Psalm 139:15-16
7 ....Isaiah 49:2
8 ....1 John 3:1
9 ....Psalm 147:3
10 ....2 Corinthians 3:18
11 ....Psalm 84:11
12 ....Psalm 91:4
13 ....Isaiah 57:2
14 ....Jeremiah 1:5
15 ....Philippians 1:9-11
16 ....2 Chronicles 7: 14
17 ....Mark 11:25
18 ....1 Corinthians 1:8
19 ....Psalm 48:14
20 ....Proverbs 2:7-8
21 ....Psalm 15:12
22 ....James 1:17
23 ....Lamentations 3:31-33
24 ....Psalm 119:1-2
25 ....Psalm 62:7
26 ....1 Peter 3:9
27 ....Proverbs 11:3
28 ....Proverbs 10:9
29 ....Psalm 41:12
30 ....1 Corinthians 3:9
31 ....Romans 12:5-6

June
1 .... Deuteronomy 31:8
2 .... Romans 8:16
3 .... Psalm 23:4
4 .... Jeremiah 33:8
5 .... 1 John 1:9
6 .... Psalm 32:1-2
7 .... Colossians 1:13-14
8 .... Psalm 86:5
9 .... Psalm 32:5
10 .... Matthew 6:14
11 .... 1 John 2:12
12 .... Hebrews 10:22-23
13 .... John 15:15
14 .... John 15:12-13
15 .... Ephesians 3:16
16 .... Proverbs 18:24
17 .... Proverbs 17:17
18 .... 1 Samuel 20:42
19 .... Psalm 130:3-4
20 .... Job 16:20-21
21 .... Proverbs 27:9
22 .... Ecclesiastes 4:9-10,12
23 .... Job 6:14
24 .... Proverbs 22:11
25 .... Luke 24:46-47
26 .... Acts 10:43
27 .... Deuteronomy 12:7
28 .... Ephesians 1:7-8
29 .... Matthew 28:30
30 .... Micah 7:18

July
1 .... 2 Samuel 7:29
2 .... Psalm 119:76
3 .... Psalm 27:1,5, 13-14
4 .... 1 Peter 5:7
5 .... Psalm 37:4
6 .... Joshua 1:8
7 .... 1 Peter 3:1-2
8 .... Proverbs 22:9
9 .... Philippians 1:6
10 .... Psalm 37:37
11 .... Proverbs 24:14
12 .... Proverbs 16:3
13 .... Proverbs 11:5
14 .... Hebrews 10:36
15 .... John 16:22
16 .... Ecclesiastes 9:7
17 .... Romans 5:2,11
18 .... Matthew 5:12
19 .... Isaiah 30:26
20 .... Luke 10:20
21 .... Psalm 96:11-13
22 .... Psalm 22:30
23 .... James 1:25
24 .... 1 John 2:17
25 .... 2 Peter 3:9
26 .... John 13:34-35
27 .... Romans 15:13
28 .... 1 Thessalonians 3:12
29 .... Hosea 2:19-20
30 .... James 3:18
31 .... Genesis 2:18

August
1 .... Proverbs 10:6
2 .... Hebrews 3:6
3 .... Psalm 34:17
4 .... Numbers 6:24,25
5 .... Proverbs 12:2
6 .... Song of Solomon 4:10
7 .... Proverbs 31:28-29
8 .... 1 John 4:18
9 .... 1 John 4:12
10 .... 1 Peter 2:25
11 .... Revelation 7:17
12 .... Hebrews 13:20-21
13 .... John 10:27-30
14 .... Galatians 4:6-7
15 .... Ephesians 5:1-2
16 .... Joshua 1:9
17 .... 1 John 5:2-4
18 .... Galatians 3:26,28

19 ....Psalms 127:3-5
20 ....Psalm 107:41
21 ....1 John 4:14-15
22 ....John 6:47
23 ....Romans 10:9-10
24 ....John 11:25-26
25 ....Hebrews 9:28
26 ....2 Corinthians 5:1
27 ....Revelation 21:27
28 ....Isaiah 41:10
29 ....Revelation 21:1, 3-4
30 ....Revelation 7:16-17
31 ....Acts 3:19

September
1 ....1 Corinthians 3:8-9
2 ....Isaiah 40:11
3 ....Psalm 113:9
4 ....Proverbs 29:17
5 ....Psalm 138:8
6 ....Jeremiah 31:3
7 .... Psalm 112:1-2
8 ....Lamentations 3:22-23
9 ....Psalm 130:5-6
10 ....Isaiah 26:8
11 ....Isaiah 51:5
12 ....Isaiah 64:4
13 ....Micah 7:7
14 ....1 Thessalonians 1:2-3
15 ....1 Corinthians 1:7
16 ....Ephesians 1:5-6
17 ....Exodus 14:14
18 ....Psalm 31:7
19 ....Isaiah 40:31
20 ....Colossians 3:23-24
21 ....Luke 16:10
22 ....Proverbs 10:4
23 ....1 Corinthians 15:58
24 ....Hebrews 4:9-10
25 ....1 John 4:16
26 ....Romans 13:8
27 ....Proverbs 17:9

28 ....Deuteronomy 33:3
29 ....Deuteronomy 33:12
30 ....Psalm 23:6

October
1 ....Psalm 115:14
2 ....Hebrews 6:10
3 ....Philippians 2:13
4 ....Proverbs 14:26
5 ....2 Corinthians 9:8
6 ....1 Corinthians 3:11-14
7 ....Genesis 1:27-28
8 ....Psalm 139:13-17
9 ....2 Timothy 1:12
10 ....Psalm 100:3
11 ....Ecclesiastes 3:11
12 ....Psalm 9:9
13 ....Psalm 34:8
14 ....Psalm 59:16
15 ....Ruth 2:12
16 ....John 17:6,11
17 ....Isaiah 43:1
18 ....Ephesians 3:12
19 ....Jeremiah 32:39
20 ....Matthew 14:25-27
21 ....Psalm 34:15
22 ....Proverbs 31:10,28
23 ....Hebrews 10:35-36
24 ....Psalm 27:1
25 ....Luke 11:9-10
26 ....Proverbs 2:1-5
27 ....Psalm 119:125
28 ....1 King 3:7-3
29 ....Proverbs 14:6
30 ....Proverbs 18:15
31 ....Galatians 6:4

November
1 ....Philippians 4:9
2 ....John 13:12-17
3 ....John 15:10
4 ....Matthew 12:50

5 ....1 John 3:21-24
6 ....Exodus 19:5
7 ....1 Kings 2:3
8 ....Jeremiah 7:23
9 ....Psalm 119:2
10 ....Colossians 2:2
11 ....James 5:7-8
12 ....Galatians 5:22-23
13 ....Psalm 38:15
14 ....Proverbs 19:11
15 ....Proverbs 25:15
16 ....Psalm 5:3
17 ....Hebrews 12:1-3
18 ....Galatians 6:9
19 ....Isaiah 26:3
20 ....Proverbs 1:5
21 ....Deuteronomy 30:19-20
22 ....Psalm 73:24
23 ....Isaiah 54:10
24 ....Psalm 94:18-19
25 ....Hebrews 11:1
26 ....Romans 8:37-39
27 ....Psalm 143:8
28 ....Proverbs 16:33
29 ....1 Chronicles 16:34
30 ....Ephesians 2:4-5

December
1 ....1 Peter 5:10-11
2 ....Romans 5:2-4
3 ....Psalm 95:6-7
4 ....Hebrews 12:28
5 ....Psalm 100:4-5
6 ....Psalm 71:22-23
7 ....Psalm 149:3-5
8 ....Revelation 4:9-11
9 ....Mark 11:24
10 ....James 5:16
11 ....Psalm 55:16-17
12 ....Matthew 7:7-8
13 ....Jeremiah 33:3
14 ....Romans 8:26

15 ....James 5:13
16 ....2 Corinthians 1:3-5
17 ....Proverbs 31:10-31
18 ....Isaiah 61:1-3
19 ....Isaiah 65:24
20 ....Matthew 18:19
21 ....Matthew 21:22
22 ....1 John 5:14-15
23 ....John 16:23-24
24 ....Psalm 145:18
25 ....Matthew 5:4
26 ....Zechariah 13:9
27 ....Jeremiah 6:16
28 ....Proverbs 19:23
29 ....Isaiah 40:28-31
30 ....Psalm 37:23-24
31 .... Philippians 4:6-7

About the Author

Evelyn Johnson-Taylor is the founder of Women of Promise, an Outreach Ministry providing an opportunity for women to encourage one another via e-mail communication and personal contact.

Evelyn J. Taylor Ministries along with Women of Promise provides counseling, mentor, coaching, prayer, Bible studies, and other outreach efforts. Our mission is to push women into a deeper relationship with Jesus Christ where she will develop a hunger to discover every promise God has made in His Word. After discovering God's promises, the women will be empowered to not only possess the promises but also be able to share God's Word and encourage other women. Evelyn has worked with pastors to establish and organize women's ministries for their churches. She and her husband Scott are both ordained ministers, and were the founders and pastors of Good News Bible Church in Gaithersburg, Maryland. Evelyn worked as a registered nurse on Capitol Hill for ten years. The Taylors now reside in Tampa, Florida, where they pastor and oversee Good News Global Ministries, Inc.

A note from Evelyn:

I have a passion for the ministry God has placed in my heart. When God called me to minister to women, I was the mother of a toddler and an infant. My first response was "God, what can I share with women? I have to focus on raising my children." God said to me very clearly, "I want you to be an example. I want young mothers to see you raising your children and loving Me."

I have tried to demonstrate with my life as a mother the value of parenting my daughters. They are still fairly young, but I have God's promise that if I am obedient to bring them up according to His Word, they too will receive the promises.

My assignment from God was to let my life be a living epistle for other women. I am to let my life be a classroom from which other women can learn. God spoke to me very clearly in regards to my assignment. My instructions were to forget about just talking the talk, and let women see me walking the walk.

God said, "Let them see you honoring your husband, let them see you taking care of your children, and let them see you obeying My Word. I want other mothers to see you investing time in your children. Be a model for others." After all, isn't that the call of every believer?

Contact Information

If you would like Evelyn to speak to your group or would like more information about this book and study guide, please contact Evelyn. She would also love to hear how God has used this book to help you in your life.

Evelyn Johnson-Taylor
www.evelynjtaylor.org
evelynjtaylor@aol.com